W9-DAG-058

Structured Exercises in

Management

Volume

5

Structured Exercises in

STRESS

Management

A Handbook for
Trainers, Educators, Group Leaders

Volume

5

Edited by
Nancy Loving Tubesing, EdD
Sandy Stewart Christian, MSW

Copyright © 1995 by Whole Person Associates Inc.

REPRODUCTION POLICY

Unless otherwise noted, your purchase of this volume entitles you to reproduce a modest quantity of the worksheets that appear in this book for your education/training activities. For this limited worksheet reproduction no special additional permission is needed. However the following statement, in total, must appear on all copies that you reproduce.

> Reproduced from *Structured Exercises in Stress Management, Volume 5,* Nancy Loving Tubesing and Sandy Stewart Christian, Editors. © 1995 Whole Person Associates, 210 W Michigan, Duluth, MN 55802.

Specific prior written permission is required from the publisher for any reproduction of a complete or adapted exercise with trainer instructions, or large-scale reproduction of worksheets, or for inclusion of material in another publication. Licensing or royalty arrangement requests for this usage must be submitted in writing and approved to prior to any such use.

For further information please write for our Permissions Guidelines and Standard Permissions Form. Permission requests must be submitted at least 30 days in advance of your scheduled printing or reproduction.

Library of Congress Cataloging in Publication Data

Structured exercises in stress management : A handbook for trainers, educators, and
   group leaders / Nancy Loving Tubesing and Sandy Stewart Christian, eds.
   192p. 23cm.
      Summary: A collection of thiry-six exercises for stress management to be used
by trainers and facilitators in group settings.
   ISBN 1-57025-016-2 (v.5 : pbk) : $29.95
      1. Stress (psychology)—Prevention, problems, exercises, etc. 2. Stress—
Psychological, prevention & control, problems. I. Title. II. Tubesing, Nancy Loving
III. Christian, Sandy Stewart
   BF575.S75S74   1986, 1990, 1994, 1994, 1995
   158'.92-dc19
83-61073

Printed in the United States of America

10 9 8 7 6 5 4 3 2 1

Published by: 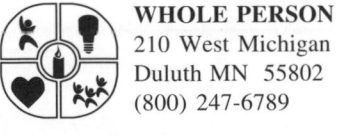 **WHOLE PERSON ASSOCIATES**
210 West Michigan
Duluth MN 55802
(800) 247-6789

PREFACE

Over a decade ago we launched an experiments in health education—the Whole Person series of **Structured Exercises in Stress Management** *and* **Structured Exercises in Wellness Promotion.** *We believed that it was time to move beyond peptalks and handouts to an experiential approach that actively involves the participant—as a whole person—in the learning process.*

What began as an experiment has become a catalyst for dramatic change in health promotion and education! **Structured Exercises** *volumes have found their way into the libraries of trainers, consultants, group workers, and health professionals around the world. We're proud that these volumes have become classics—the resource of choice for planning stress management and wellness promotion programs.*

Our purpose in publishing this series was to foster inter-professional networking and to provide a framework though which we can all share our most effective ideas with each other. As you will soon discover, we scoured the country looking for the most innovative, effective teaching designs used by the most creative consultants and trainers in business, health care, and social services, then included some of their most imaginative ideas in this volume.

Many of the exercises we designed ourselves and refined in hundreds of workshops we've conducted over the past twenty years. Some are new combinations of time-tested group process activities. Others were submitted by people like you who continually strive to add the creative touch to their teaching.

The layout of **Structured Exercises** *is designed for easy photocopying of worksheets, handouts, and preparation notes. Please take advantage of our generous policy for reproduction—but also please be fair to the creative individuals who have so generously shared their ideas with you.*

☞ *You may duplicate worksheets and handouts for use in training or educational events—as long as you use the proper citation as indicated on the copyright page. Please also give written credit to the original contributor. Whenever we've been able to track down the source of an idea, we've noted it. Please do the same when you share these ideas with others.*

☞ *However, all materials in this volume are still protected by copyright. Prior written permission from Whole Person Press is required if you* plan large scale reproduction or distribution of any portion of this book. If you wish to include any material or adaptation in another publication, you must have permission in writing before proceeding. Please send us your request and proposal at least thirty days in advance.

Structured Exercises are now available in two convenient formats. This small-format softcover version is produced with a new book binding process that stays open on your desk or podium for easy reference, and lies flat on the photocopier for quick duplication of worksheets.

Many trainers enjoy the wide margins and larger type of the full-size looseleaf format, which provides plenty of space for you to add your own workshop designs, examples, chalktalk notes, and process reminders for your presentations. The looseleaf version also includes a complete package of camera-ready worksheet masters for easy reproduction of professional-looking handouts.

☞ See page 155 in the Resources section for complete descriptions and ordering information for worksheet masters and companion volumes of the **Stress** and **Wellness** series in softcover and looseleaf formats.

We are grateful to the many creative trainers who have go generously shared their "best" with you in this volume (see page 150) as well as others in the series. We hope that the ideas here stimulate your own creative juices.

So, go ahead. Strive to bring your teaching alive in new ways. Expand your stress management approach. Continue to touch and motivate people with learning experiences that engage and challenge them as whole persons.

Then let us know what works well for you. We'd love to consider your new ideas for inclusion in a future volume so that we can carry on the tradition of providing this international exchange of innovative teaching designs.

Duluth MN   Nancy Loving Tubesing
June 1995   Sandy Stewart Christian

INTRODUCTION

Stress is a fact of life—and from the board room to the emergency room to the living room, people are searching for ways to manage stress more positively.

Structured Exercises in Stress Management, Volume 5 offers you 36 designs you can use for helping people move beyond information to implementation. Each exercise is structured to involve people creatively in the learning process, whatever the setting and time constraints, whatever the sophistication of the audience. To aid you in the selection of appropriate exercises, they are grouped into six broad categories:

> *Icebreakers:* These short (5–20 minutes) and lively exercises are designed to introduce people to each other and to the subject of stress management. Try combining an icebreaker with an exercise from the assessment or management section for an instant evening program.

> *Stress Assessments:* These exercises explore the symptoms, sources, and dynamics of stress. All the processes help people examine the impact of stress in their lives. You'll find a mixture of shorter assessments (30–60 minutes) and major theme developers (60–90 minutes). Any exercise can easily be contracted or expanded to fit your purpose.

> *Management Strategies:* Each of these processes explores the issue of overall strategies for dealing with the stress of life. Participants evaluate their strengths and weaknesses and identify skills for future development.

> *Skill Developers:* Each volume in this handbook series will focus on a few coping skills in more depth. The five exercises in this section highlight relaxation, surrender, laughter, and interpersonal contact skills.

> *Action Planning/Closure:* These exercises help participants draw together their insights and determine the actions they wish to take on their own behalf. Some also suggest rituals that bring closure to the group process.

> *Energizers:* The energizers are designed to perk up the group whenever fatigue sets in. Sprinkle them throughout your program to illustrate skills or concepts. Try one for a change of pace-everyone's juices (including yours!) will be flowing again in 5–10 minutes.

The format is designed for easy use. You'll find that each exercise is described completely, including: goals, group size, time frame, materials needed, step-by-step process instructions and variations.

☞ *Special instructions for the trainer and scripts to be read to the group are typed in italics.*

✔ Questions to ask the group are preceded by a check.

➤ Directions for group activities are indicated by an arrow.

● Mini-lecture notes are preceded by a bullet.

Although the processes are primarily described for large groups (25–100 people) workshop settings, most of the exercises work just as well with small groups, and many are appropriate for individual therapy or personal reflection.

If you are teaching in the workshop or large group setting, we believe that the use of small discussion groups is the most potent learning structure available to you. We've found that groups of four persons each provide ample air time and a good variety of interaction. If possible, let groups meet together two or three different times during the learning experience before forming new groups.

These personal sharing groups allow people to make positive contact with each other and encourage them to personalize their experience in depth. On evaluation, some people will say, "Drop this," others will say, "Give us more small group time," but most will report that the time you give them to share with each other becomes the heart of the workshop.

If you are working with an intact group of twelve people or less, you may want to keep the whole group together for process and discussion time rather than divide into the suggested four or six person groups.

Each trainer has personal strengths, biases, pet concepts, and processes. We expect and encourage you to expand and modify what you find here to accommodate your style. Adjust the exercises as you see fit. Bring these designs to life for your participants by inserting your own content and examples into your teaching. Experiment!

And when you come up with something new, let us know . . .

CONTENTS

STRESS ASSESSMENTS

MANAGEMENT STRATEGIES

SKILL BUILDERS

PLANNING/CLOSURE

GROUP ENERGIZERS

RESOURCES

Icebreakers

145 INTRODUCTIONS 10

In these two creative icebreakers, participants get acquainted as they share graphic representations of their current stress and goals for the session (**Symbols**) and identify stresses of their birth month (**Birthday Party**).

GOALS

To get acquainted.

To identify goals for the learning experience.

GROUP SIZE

Unlimited.

TIME FRAME

5–15 minutes

MATERIALS NEEDED

Symbols: two large, self-adhesive plain white nametags for each participant; pens or fine-point colored markers for each participant.

Introduction A. SYMBOLS

1) The trainer gives each participant two blank nametags and a pen or colored marker.

2) The trainer explains that individuals will get acquainted by using hand-drawn symbols to represent their current stress and their goals for the workshop.

   ➤ Fold the first name tag in half vertically.

   ➤ Unfold it and use the left half to draw a symbol of yourself and the current stress in your life.

   ☞ *Stimulate group member's ideas by provocative questions. Do you see yourself as carrying a backpack full of rocks? Are you juggling too many balls? Or running a marathon?*

   ➤ On the right side of your nametag draw a symbol of your goal for the workshop.

   ➤ Ask yourself, what do I want or need from this workshop?

➤ What symbol would portray this positive change for me?

➤ Be creative and playful.

➤ Use the second nametag to write your first name in large letters.

3) When everyone has finished drawing, the trainer asks group members to stand up, put on both nametags, and then follow these steps:

➤ Move around the room and find a person you would like to know better.

➤ When you have a partner, introduce yourself by showing your symbols and explaining a bit about your current stress and your goals for the session.

4) After about 2 or 3 minutes, the trainer asks participants to find new partners and introduce themselves using their symbols.

5) After the second pair has finished their introductions, the trainer ends the exercise by welcoming all participants and encouraging them to continue wearing their nametags during the rest of the workshop.

VARIATIONS

■ If time is limited, participants could introduce themselves to just one other person. If there is more time, group members could introduce themselves to several people, moving quickly from person to person, until four to six people have been met.

■ The trainer could use the goal symbols as a catalyst for large group discussion about workshop goals. People can share their goals with the large group, write them on a large newsprint, and then negotiate or clarify final goals with the group.

Introduction B. BIRTHDAY PARTY

1) The trainer invites participants to get together in groups by the month of their birthday.

☞ *Designate 12 locations for gathering. It the groups are extremely unbalanced, combine 2 small groups. If the total number of participants is less than 20, divide by birthday quarters (Jan/Feb/ Mar, Apr/May/June, etc).*

2) The trainer gives instructions for the introductions.

> ➤ Go around the group and introduce yourselves, telling your birthday and one stress that is common during that month.

> ➤ When all have been introduced, discuss together additional stresses that often occur during your mutual birthday month.

3) When all groups have made introductions, the trainer interrupts and invites participants to shift their focus to coping strategies.

> ➤ Brainstorm together a list of coping resources or strategies that are ideal for your birth month.

4) The trainer reconvenes the large group and solicits examples of stressors and coping strategies generated in the discussion, and uses these resources as a bridge to the next learning experience.

VARIATIONS

■ Groups could make posters for their months and hang them around the room as a monthly guide to stress management.

■ Teach the *Humming Breath,* p 122, technique here, and hum a rousing *Happy Birthday* to all.

146 BADGE OF MY PROFESSION

Participants identify work-related stress and healthy aspects of their jobs to portray on an ID badge.

GOALS

To explore job stresses and identify desired changes.

To affirm personal resources for coping.

To get acquainted.

GROUP SIZE

Unlimited.

TIME FRAME

15–20 minutes

MATERIALS NEEDED

ID Badge worksheet; 24" pieces of yarn or string; several rolls of scotch tape.

PROCESS

1) The trainer distributes **ID Badge** worksheets and announces that participants are going to create an ID badge that will grant them entrance to this learning experience.

2) The trainer gives instructions for filling out the form.

> ☞ *Pause between each instruction until most people are finished.*

➤ On the left side of the badge, in the box labeled "ID," print:
> ➣ Your name.
> ➣ Three adjectives that would help identify you.
> ➣ Your job title.

➤ In *Section A* list four or five of the **stresses** you experience in your job.

➤ In *Section B* identify three **healthy aspects** of your job.

➤ In *Section C* identify two **changes** that you know would make your job less stressful.

©1995 Whole Person Press 210 W Michigan Duluth MN 55802   (800) 247-6789

3) The trainer invites participants to put on their ID badges, using the yarn and tape to hang the worksheets around their necks.

4) The trainer gives instructions for the mixer.

> As soon as your ID badge is in place, start milling around the room checking out your fellow workers.

> Find two other people whose job stress issues seem similar to yours.

> As soon as you have found a group of three, spend 5 minutes describing to each other the stresses of your job that particularly bother you.

5) After about 5 minutes, the trainer interrupts and asks participants to shift their focus to a discussion of the healthy aspects of their job and how those healthy dimensions may help them cope with stress at work.

6) After about 5 minutes, the trainer interrupts again and directs triads to pair up with a neighboring threesome to form groups of six.

Once groups are settled, the trainer gives instructions for introductions.

> Take turns introducing yourselves by saying something about the changes you think would make your job less stressful.

> Take about one minute each to share your changes.

7) The trainer reconvenes the large group and solicits examples that will help make a bridge to the next content segment.

VARIATIONS

■ After *Step 6* add another round of sharing in sextets, this time asking participants to identify what they want to learn from this class/session/ workshop.

■ The ID questions in this exercise could be adapted to fit a variety of content material by changing the questions.

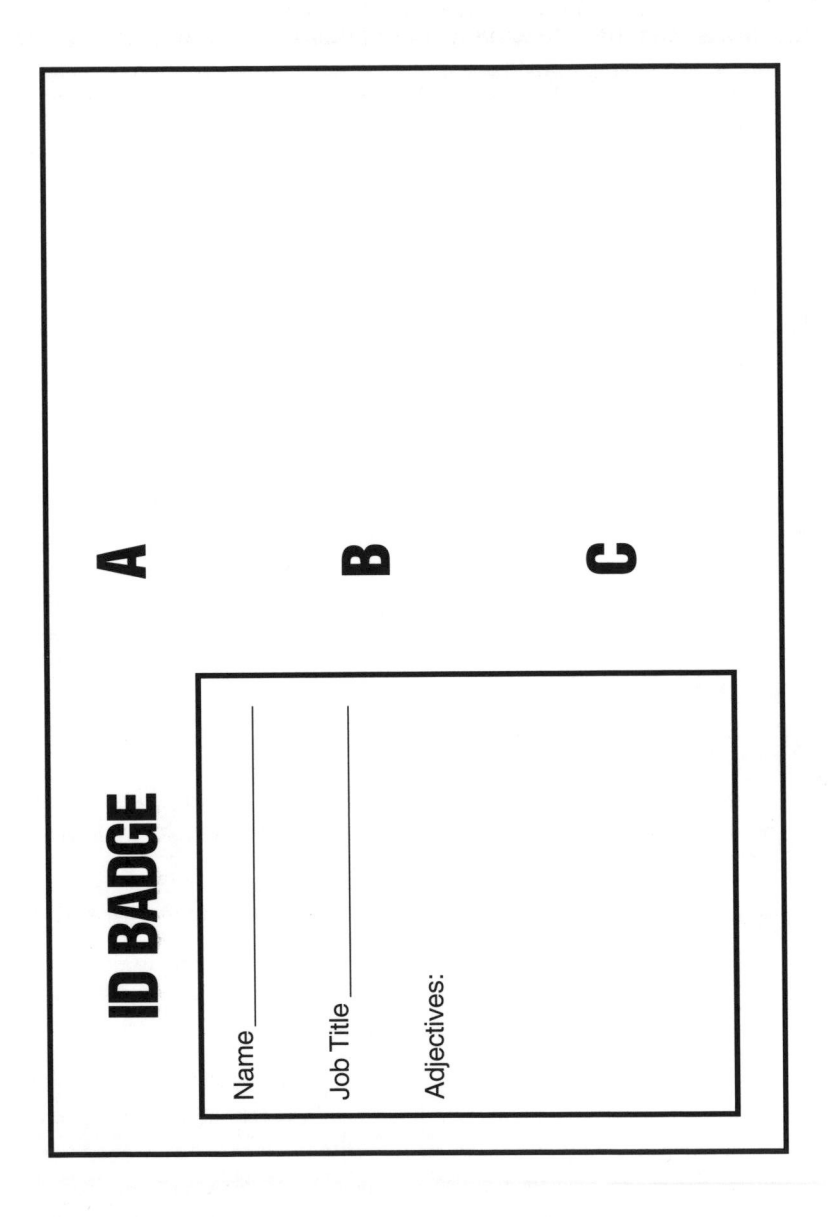

©1995 Whole Person Press 210 W Michigan Duluth MN 55802   (800) 247-6789

147 NAMETAG QUESTIONS

In this intriguing mixer, participants mill around the group and answer questions about stress which are printed on each other's nametags.

GOALS

To get acquainted.

To stimulate thinking about personal styles of stress management.

GROUP SIZE

Unlimited.

TIME FRAME

15–20 minutes

MATERIALS NEEDED

For each participant: a nametag (pressure sensitive or 3x5 note card) with a unique question about stress management written or typed on it (see list on p 9). Horn or harmonica to use for signaling time to change partners.

PROCESS

☞ *Write a stress question for each participant on a nametag prior to the learning session. You can modify or add questions to suit the specific agendas of your participants. If you have more people than questions, make more! Or allow duplicate questions, but not duplicate answers.*

1) The trainer makes sure that all participants are wearing a nametag with a stress question on it, and that the nametag is easily visible.

2) She then announces that participants will have the opportunity to get to know 10 other participants. She asks everyone to stand up, move around, and then pair up with someone they do not know.

3) When everyone has a partner, she explains the next steps of the exercise.

   ➤ You will have about one minute to answer the question on your partner's nametag.

   ➤ When you hear the horn blown, move on to a new partner, answer the question on their nametag, and listen to your partner's answer to the question on your nametag.

©1995 Whole Person Press 210 W Michigan Duluth MN 55802   (800)247-6789

➤ Continue to move to a new partner each time the horn blows, until you have talked with 10 different people.

4) When the introductions are completed, the trainer solicits general insights or gems of wisdom gleaned from group members' discussions with other participants. She ties these ideas in with the agenda of the learning session and then moves on into the designated topic.

VARIATIONS

■ Participants form groups of 10 people and answer the nametag questions of everyone in their group.

■ As part of *Step 4* ask each participant to recall and write down the ten different answers they heard to the question on their nametag. Invite those who wish to share their list with the whole group to do so.

TRAINER'S NOTES

Submitted by Krysta Kavenaugh.

STRESS QUESTIONS

How does (did) your mother cope with stress?

What was your favorite coping stategy as a child?

What is the most common stress of your profession?

What is the quickest, most effective tension reliever you know?

What is one stress reducer you use that has potentially harmful side effects?

What effect has the stress in your life had on your health?

If you could eliminate one stress from your environment, what would you get rid of?

In your work setting, what are some of the stresses you can't control?

What's your worst stress habit?

What's your favorite way to unwind?

What is one stress you remember from childhood?

What are some of the special stresses of your current age?

What is the best stress management advice you've ever received?

What are some stresses unique to your gender?

Describe a typical stress in your current family or family of origin.

What is most stressful for you in attending a learning experience like this?

What is your favorite book about stress management?

What part of your body feels stress first?

How is your stress related to your religious/spiritual beliefs or practices?

What comforts you when you are hassled and frustrated?

What challenges are you currently facing that are causing you stress?

What changes have been stressful for you in the last year?

If you had $500 to spend on stress management, what would you do with the money?

Who is your model for healthy stress management and why?

What are your personal goals for stress management?

How do you maintain a positive outlook in life?

How do you stop worrying?

How does stress affect your performance at work?

What are some of the stressful aspects of your personal relationships?

148 ONE MINUTE AUTOBIOGRAPHIES

Participants tell their life story in one minute, using an easy, open-ended process.

GOALS

To get acquainted.

To share important parts of personal history with other group members.

GROUP SIZE

Works best with groups of 8–16 people. Divide larger audiences into groups of this size.

TIME FRAME

10–20 minutes

MATERIALS NEEDED

Big clock with a second hand; newsprint poster with instructions.

PROCESS

1) The trainer invites participants get acquainted by telling short auto-biographies of their lives.

> ➤ Stand up, find a partner and exchange names.

>> ☞ *Pause until all have partners.*

> ➤ Each of you has one minute to tell part of your life story.

>> ➣ Select any time of life that you want to focus on.

>> ➣ Don't worry about how the story will come out. Just make it up as you go, without thinking ahead. Whatever you say is fine.

> ➤ Use these four phrases as paragraph starters:

>> ➣ When I was . . .
>> ➣ At that time my dreams . . .
>> ➣ And I did . . .
>> ➣ And now . . .

>>> ☞ *Demonstrate with your own one-minute autobiography using the format. You may want to post these questions in a highly visible spot.*

> When the first person has talked for one minute, switch roles, so the second person can tell your story.

2) When all have finished their stories, the trainer instructs each pair to join with another pair to form a quartet, for another round of autobiographies focusing on **careers**.

> Select a timekeeper.

> You each have one minute to tell a **vocational** autobiography, using the following format:
   > When I was young . . .
   > Then my dreams . . .
   > And I did . . .
   > And now . . .

3) After everyone has had the opportunity to tell their vocational story, the trainer asks each quartet to join another quartet, forming octets, for another round of autobiographies focusing on **stress**.

> Select a timekeeper.

> Each person has one minute to tell your **stress autobiography**, using the same format:
   > When I was . . .
   > Then my dreams . . .
   > And I did . . .
   > And now . . .

4) When group members have finished their stress autobiographies, the trainer announces that the time is up and brings closure to the exercise by inviting general comments from the group about their experiences in this exercise.

VARIATIONS

■ Tailor the focus for the autobiographies to the agenda and interests of your group: eg, a corporate autobiography, fitness autobiography, health autobiography, educational autobiography, friendship autobiography, coping autobiography, crisis autobiography, spiritual autobiography, etc.

■ With a small group (less than twenty participants), keep the whole group together for sharing **stress** autobiographies in *Step 3*.

149 PACE SETTERS

Participants choose a vehicle that represents their pace of life and use this model to introduce themselves to other group members.

GOALS

To reflect on stress and the pace of life.

To get acquainted.

GROUP SIZE

Unlimited.

TIME FRAME

5–10 minutes

PROCESS

1) The trainer introduces the issue of stress and the pace of life with a few appropriate comments.

   ● One common source of stress is the pace of life. For some folks, the pace is too slow, and they face the stress of boredom or stagnation. For others, the hectic, even frantic pace of life is stressful. Most of us fall somewhere between most of the time.

2) The trainer invites participants to reflect on the pace of their lives in recent days, weeks, or months.

   ➤ Choose a vehicle that represents your pace for the last few weeks. Be imaginative.

   ☞ *Give lots of examples from the list below.*

   ➤ Introduce yourself to the group, giving your name, a description of your pace vehicle, and a brief explanation of why it fits you so well.

   ☞ *To demonstrate, introduce yourself to the group using an appropriate vehicle and explanation.*

3) The trainer connects the concept of *pace of life* to the group learning goals, and moves to the next agenda item.

PACE SETTER LIST

Indy car	stock car	motor scooter
armored car	camper	chariot
dog cart	stage coach	wheelbarrow
pram	tractor	bulldozer
bookmobile	ambulance	tanker
cart	covered wagon	little red wagon
horse and buggy	carriage	baby buggy
stroller	bike	trike
scooter	skateboard	garbage truck
fire engine	hearse	motorcycle
moped	sports car	roadster
convertible	hot rod	jeep
limousine	taxi	side car
jalopy	wrecker	street sweeper
snow plow	freight train	Amtrack
subway	commuter train	express train
pullman	streetcar	trolley
double decker bus	van	bus
pickup truck	4 x 4	16-wheeler

©1995 Whole Person Press 210 W Michigan Duluth MN 55802   (800) 247-6789

150 TON OF BRICKS

In this amusing and weighty exercise participants get acquainted while identifying concrete stresses in their lives.

GOALS

To get acquainted.

To identify life stresses.

GROUP SIZE

Can be adapted to fit all groups.

TIME FRAME

15–20 minutes

MATERIALS NEEDED

One masonry building brick for each small group.

PROCESS

1) The trainer begins by asking participants to form small groups based on construction materials.

   ☞ *Be creative as you choose process for dividing into groups. Divide by type of home or apartments you live in now (brick, concrete, wood frame, aluminum siding). Adjust as necessary so there are 5–8 people in each group. With less than 12 people, keep the whole group together or divide in half by apartment vs house.*

2) After everyone has joined a group, the trainer gives each group a brick and introduces the exercise with a brief chalktalk.

   ● **Stress often feels like a heavy load that we carry around.** This burden can weigh us down, sap our energy and make our shoulders, neck, head, and back ache. Sometimes we describe the stress of bad news by saying, "It hit me like a load of bricks."

   ● **Multiple demands on our time and energy are like weights** that we juggle day after day. It can be exhausting to balance all of the pieces in our lives.

3) After this brief warm-up talk, the trainer explains the process for this introductory exercise.

> ➤ Introduce yourself to the group by holding the brick, stating your name, and talking about these three things:

>> ➤ What stress is weighing you down?

>> ➤ What are you juggling or carrying around that causes you stress?

>> ➤ What do you need to shed?

> ➤ Take two minutes each to talk about yourself.

> ➤ Select a group member to be a timekeeper.

> ➤ When the first speaker is finished, pass the brick to the next person.

> ➤ Go around the group until all people have had an opportunity to introduce themselves.

4) When all introductions are completed, the trainer concludes the exercise by collecting the bricks and stacking them in a pile in a corner of the room, joking that participants can now relax and let go of their stresses for the duration of the workshop.

VARIATIONS

■ Instead of bricks, use rocks. Participants take a bag and go on a quick rock collecting walk (if the environment is appropriate) to gather a bag of rocks that represents their current stressload. Individuals then talk about their rocks in small groups.

Submitted by Pat Miller.

TRAINER'S NOTES

Stress
Assessments

151 THE HARDINESS FACTOR

Using a test for hardiness developed by the researchers who coined the concept, participants assess their ability to resist stress by measuring three key personal traits: challenge, commitment, and control.

GOALS

To measure personal hardiness.

To explore ways to become more stress-resistant.

GROUP SIZE

Unlimited. May also be used with individuals.

TIME FRAME

30–40 minutes

MATERIALS NEEDED

One copy of the **Hardiness Questionnaire** for each participant; large sheets of newsprint labeled **commitment**, **control**, and **challenge**; magic markers; and masking tape.

PROCESS

1) The trainer introduces the concept of hardiness, or stress resistance, and invites participants to make a *pretest* assessment of their own hardiness level, using a human continuum.

    ☞ *The front or back wall usually makes a good place to line up. Designate which end is **extremely hardy** and which end is **not very hardy**.*

   ➤ Stand up and place yourself at some position on this hardiness continuum, according to the degree of hardiness you consider your-self to have.

   ➤ When everyone is in position, turn to the person next to you and briefly explain why you placed yourself where you did.

2) After 2 minutes the trainer asks participants to return to their seats, thanking everyone for having the courage to respond to this challenging introduction and adding that taking this kind of risk is a trait of hardy people.

©1995 Whole Person Press 210 W Michigan Duluth MN 55802   (800) 247-6789

3) The trainer expands the idea of hardiness in a chalktalk.

- **The quality of hardiness enables some people to deal with stress better than others.** University of Chicago researchers Suzanne Ouelette Kabasa and Salvator Maddi studied 259 male executives and found that the hardy personality is the most stress-resistant. The "hardy" people studied were one-half as prone to illness as others, regardless of how many life events they experienced.

- Hardy people differ from the less-hardy on three personality traits.

  ○ **Challenge. For hardy types, change is viewed as a challenge**, not as a threat or an unending stream of hassles. A satisfying life is seen as a series of problems or puzzles to solve. Problems are opportunities for growth and mastery. Instead of avoiding and resisting change, hardy individuals expect change, are open to it, and energized by it.

  ○ **Commitment. Hardy people are engaged with life**, rather than alienated or detached from it. They are actively involved in their work, family, and social life. They have a mission or purpose in life, and a strong belief that what they do is meaningful. They do not let fear hold them back. They take risks, commit themselves to their deepest desires, and *Go for it!* in ways they want. They live life to the fullest, and try to *Be all they can be.*

  ○ **Control. Hardy individuals feel a sense of control over their lives**, rather than feeling of powerless. Hardy individuals believe they can have a real impact on their surroundings. They don't wait for bad things to happen; instead, they anticipate change, plan for it, and take actions to enhance their performance in the present. This involves setting priorities, managing time, and investing energy on things they can control.

4) The trainer distributes **Hardiness Questionnaires** and announces the *posttest*, in which participants will assess their hardiness in more detail, using a measurement tool developed by the researcher who first discovered the hardy personality traits.

  ➤ Read the 12 items and write down how much you agree or disagree with each statement, using a 4-point scale.

  ➤ Write your number to the left of the statement.
  - 0 = strongly disagree
  - 1 = mildly disagree
  - 2 = mildly agree
  - 3 = strongly agree

5) When everyone has completed the questionnaire, the trainer explains how to score it.

> ➤ These questions measure control, challenge, and commitment. For half the questions, a high score (like 3, "strongly agree") indicates hardiness; for the other half, a low score (disagreement) does.

> ➤ To get your score on **control**, **commitment** and **challenge**, you need to make a sequence of calculations

>> ➤ Add your scores from *Statements A and G*. Put that sum in the space labeled "A+G" at the bottom of the worksheet.

>> ➤ Add your scores from *Statements B and H*. Put that sum in the space labeled "B+H" at the bottom.

>> ➤ Now calculate your **control** score by subtracting the second sum from the first and writing it in the space provided.

> ➤ Repeat this process to determine your **commitment** and **challenge** scores.

> ➤ Then add your scores in commitment, control, and challenge together to get a score for **total hardiness**.

6) When all participants have calculated their scores, the trainer explains the ranges.

>> ➤ A total score of 10–18 shows a hardy personality.
>> ➤ 0–9 indicates moderate hardiness.
>> ➤ Below 0 suggests low hardiness.

7) The trainer posts newsprint posters labeled **commitment**, **control**, and **challenge** at three locations around the room, and instructs participants to divide into three groups.

> ➤ Join the group that corresponds to the trait in which you had the highest score.

> ➤ In order to balance group size, individuals who scored equally high in more than one trait should join the smaller group.

8) The trainer gives each group magic markers, and asks them to act as a panel of experts on their strongest trait.

> ➤ The person with the highest commitment score will be the group reporter, and should write group ideas on the newsprint.

> ➤ Since you are the experts on this trait, brainstorm as many ideas as you can imagine for a person to become **hardier** in this dimension of personality.

> ➤ You have 5 minutes to make your list.

9) After 5 minutes, the trainer invites group reporters to bring their lists to the front of the room, display them, and read the ideas to the large group.

10) When all three groups have given their reports, the trainer thanks them again for their hardiness in responding to this challenge, then summarizes important ideas presented and incorporates them into a closing chalktalk/challenge.

- **Learn to thrive on challenge.** Review your past successes and affirm your ability to achieve goals, cope with change, and learn from mistakes. Adopt the role of curious learner in new situations. Focus on enjoying the process of discovery.

- **Pay attention to committment.** Reflect on the meaning of your work, personal relationships, and leisure activities. What do you value and enjoy? If this is unclear, try listing everything you do in a day and rank each activity on a scale on 1–10, with high scores given to activities you love. Make sure you invest time and energy in activities you value or enjoy. Volunteer to help others at home, church, or in the community.

- **Focus on things you can control.** Take charge of your attitude and actions. Decide what you can realistically accomplish today. Make a plan of activity that is clear, constructive, and current. Spend time preparing for important events. And remember to participate in some form of physical relaxation or method of unwinding everyday. This will reduce stress, and help you stay healthy and able to focus on the present moment.

VARIATIONS

- For a longer workshop on hardiness, combine this assessment with processes that focus on **control** (*Yesterday, Today, and Tomorrow,* p 66 or *Pick Your Battles,* p 34), **commitment** (*Expanding Your Circles,* **Wellness 4**, p 71 or *Life and Death Questions,* **Wellness 2**, p 85), and **challenge** (*Silver Linings,* p 55).

Hardiness factor research was originally done by Suzanne Oulette Kobasa.

HARDINESS QUESTIONNAIRE

Below are 12 items similar to those that appeared in the original hardiness questionnaire. Evaluating someone's hardiness requires more than this quick test. But this simple exercise should give you some idea of how hardy you are.

Write down how much you agree or disagree with the following statements, using this scale:

> 0 = strongly disagree   2 = mildly agree
> 1 = mildly disagree   3 = strongly agree

____ **A.** Trying my best at work makes a difference.

____ **B.** Trusting to fate is sometimes all I can do in a relationship.

____ **C.** I often wake up eager to start on the day's projects.

____ **D.** Thinking of myself as a free person leads to great frustration and difficulty.

____ **E.** I would be willing to sacrifice financial security in my work if something really challenging came along.

____ **F.** It bothers me when I have to deviate from the routine or schedule I've set for myself.

____ **G.** An average citizen can have an impact on politics.

____ **H.** Without the right breaks, it is hard to be successful in my field.

____ **I.** I know why I am doing what I'm doing at work.

____ **J.** Getting close to people puts me at risk of being obligated to them.

____ **K.** Encountering new situations is an important priority in my life.

____ **L.** I really don't mind when I have nothing to do.

_____	minus	_____	=	_____
A + G		B + H		control score
_____	minus	_____	=	_____
C + I		D + J		commitment score
_____	minus	_____	=	_____
E + K		F + L		challenge score

Total Hardiness Score   _____

*The **Hardiness Questionnaire** is taken from Suzanne Ouellette Kobasa's article "How Hardy Are You?" (**American Health Magazine** September 1984, p 64–77). Reprinted with permission from the publisher.*

©1995 Whole Person Press 210 W Michigan Duluth MN 55802   (800) 247-6789

152 LIFE TRAP 5: SUPERWOMAN

In this multi-phased exercise, women explore stresses unique to women and the trap of trying *to do it all*. Participants assess their stress symptoms and explore three areas of special concern to women (guilt, self-esteem, and entitlement) and plan strategies for reducing Superwoman stress.

GOALS

To identify and validate stresses unique to women.

To explore the effects of stress on physical, mental, emotional, spiritual, and relational health.

To develop tools for raising self-esteem.

To empower women to take actions to reduce their stress.

GROUP SIZE

Unlimited.

TIME FRAME

60–90 minutes

MATERIALS NEEDED

Blank paper, one copy of **Superwoman Stress Symptoms**, **Bill of Rights**, and **Stop Superwoman Stress** worksheets for each participant; large newsprint, easel and marker.

PROCESS

☞ *This is a five-part exercise:*
   A.   *Stress and the Superwoman Myth (10–15 min)*
   B.   *Guilt and Expectations: Reflection and Sharing (10–15 min)*
   C.   *Stress and Self-Esteem: Chalktalk and Affirmation (5–20 min)*
   D.   *Stress and Entitlement: Reflection and Declarations (15–20 min)*
   E.   *Strategies for Change (15 min)*

At the beginning of this exercise you might want to play the theme song from the movie **Superman** *(available in most music stores) to set a playful and lively mood.*

©1995 Whole Person Press 210 W Michigan Duluth MN 55802   (800) 247-6789

A. Stress Symptoms and Superwoman Myths (10–15 min)

1) The trainer invites participants to brainstorm a list of all the things that stress them as women, and writes these stressors on newsprint.

2) The trainer weaves group responses into a chalktalk on old and new myths about supermoms and superwomen, emphasizing the unique stresses that these myths create for women.

- **Supermom has become Superwoman.** Many women grew up with the old myths of Supermoms who were loving housewives dressed in gingham aprons, sending their children off to school with borax-washed, fresh smelling clothes and cute character faces cut into their Wonderbread sandwiches. These old myths linger on, but are being replaced by images of the new Superwoman who **does it all**. She has an exciting career, a loving family, and looks like a fashion model.

- **The modern Superwoman myth.** Columnist Ellen Goodman gave this description of a typical day in the life of our modern Superwoman: She rises at 6:00 am, meditates for half an hour, wakes up her 2.3 kids, feeds them a Grade A nutritious breakfast (which they eat!), sends them off to school, puts on a $600 Anne Klein suit, goes to her $125,000 job, which is creative and socially useful, runs six miles on her lunch hour, spends a wonderful hour of genuine quality time with her children after school, then cooks a gourmet meal in her spotless designer kitchen. While cooking supper she discusses economic trends with her husband and then, during family mealtime, continues to relate to her husband and children about meaningful topics. After the children are tucked in bed, she spends more quality time with her husband, and ends the evening with several hours of passionate lovemaking with multiple orgasms. She then has a good night's sleep and in the morning wakes refreshed and eager to start all over again.

- **Can we have it all?** Our culture perpetuates the myth that woman can and should have it all—but only by **doing it all.** We can have an intimate relationship, a career, children, money, success, beauty, wisdom, friendships, adventure, material comforts, a clean and attractive house, and anything we want—if only we are willing to work for it.

- **Being Superwoman is stressful.** Women have taken on men's roles and values, but they have not let go of traditional roles. Women compete and perform in the business world, but still assume primary responsibility for caring for the home and children. This is true regardless of marital status, education, or career. No wonder women are exhausted!

● **Women's dual responsibilities are stressful.** Many women are stressed, resentful, driven, and guilt-ridden, yet think that this is normal and rarely question their dual responsibilities. Divorced, widowed, and single women have no choice but to do the best they can to juggle work and family responsibilities. Women with partners are often reluctant to asks partners to share more household chores, because of the cultural belief that family is the woman's primary responsibility.

● **Stress affects every woman.** Regardless of whether a woman works full or part-time, or is a full-time homemaker, stress is ever present. Women who work full-time feel guilty for not doing more at home or spending more time with spouses and children. Those who work part-time are dissatisfied with their performance at work and home. And full-time homemakers often feel guilty for not contributing to the family income or for not developing a career.

● **Women have special stress.** Women experience the same stresses that men do, but have additional physiological and psychological stresses. Women have physiological stresses of PMS, menstruation, menopause, pregnancy, childbirth, and osteoporosis, plus psychological pressures of having to manage dual role conflicts, a chronic feeling of guilt for never having done enough, an overload of responsibilities at home, and a lack of social support for carrying out these demanding and often conflicting roles.

Besides the usual stress-related diseases that affect both men and women (heart attacks, ulcers, colitis, hypertension), women suffer from predominately female illnesses of anorexia, bulimia, post-partum depression, breast cancer, uterine and cervical cancer, and low self-esteem.

● **Stress is deadly.** Symptoms of stress in women are less likely to be taken seriously by physicians, yet chronic stress is just as deadly for women as it is for men. For this reason, it is important for women to recognize their stress, take steps to lower stress, and find a way to balance care for others with self-care.

3) The trainer distributes copies of the **Superwoman Stress Symptoms** worksheet, and guides participants through an assessment of the symptoms of stress they are experiencing.

➤ Stress is a whole person phenomenon.

➤ Look over the diagram and circle all symptoms that you have experienced recently in each category: physical, mental, emotional, spiritual, and relational.

➤ If you are having symptoms that are not listed, write them in the appropriate area of your worksheet.

➤ Place a star beside any symptoms which you think are related to your role as a woman or Superwoman.

➤ Circle any symptoms that are especially worrisome to you.

4) The trainer encourages participants to pay attention to their stress symptoms and use them as an SOS for needed change.

B. Guilt and Expectations: Reflection and Sharing (10–15 min)

5) The trainer conducts a quick survey of the roles being played by women in the audience by asking a series of questions, and asking group members to respond to each question affirmatively by standing up.

✔ How many of you are currently working outside the home?

✔ How many of you are currently married or living with a significant other?

✔ How many of you are parents?

✔ How many of you engage in regular volunteer work?

✔ How many of you are single parents or the sole providers of your household?

✔ How many of you are caring for aging parents?

✔ How many of you would describe yourself as tired or exhausted?

6) The trainer comments on the composition of the group, making the point that if participants answered "yes" to any of the questions, the chances are that they are experiencing some of the stresses created by our Superwoman culture.

7) The trainer explains that a common stress for women is guilt about not meeting Superwoman expectations.

● **Guilt is an emotion, not a fact.** It is a feeling of regret or remorse about actions taken or not taken. It is the result of internalized shoulds and should nots. Women judge themselves guilty when they cannot meet the high standards set by themselves or others—even when they are unrealistic.

● **Studies have shown that women experience guilt more often** than men, especially regarding child care and overall performance as a parent. This suggests that women may assume an emotional responsibility for the well-being of children that is different from that of men.

8) The trainer passes out blank paper to participants and guides them

through a process of reflecting on their own guilt-stress.

➤ Think about the little voice inside of you, nagging you about what you should or should not have done.

➤ Write down all of the things that you are feeling guilty about.

➤ List as many things as you can in two minutes, without censoring your thoughts.

9) The trainer instructs participants to pair up with another woman in the group and share their lists.

➤ Each person has 2 minutes to share your guilt list.

10) The trainer solicits examples from group members of the kinds of things they are feeling guilty about. She records these ideas on a large sheet of newsprint.

11) In a short chalktalk, the trainer explains how this guilt adds to stress.

● **Stress is a response to perceived demands.** If women are overloaded with internal and external demands, their stress will build. When attempts to meet these demands fail (or succeed!), women may feel guilty about the consequences of both failure and success.

● **Superwomen stress themselves.** When we see Superwoman expectations as demands, we push ourselves to do more and more, better and better. If this is prolonged, we can develop stress symptoms or illness.

C. Stress and Self-Esteem (5–20 min)

12) The trainer continues the chalktalk, connecting guilt and self-esteem to Superwoman stress.

● **Superwoman stress can erode self-esteem.** The late Virginia Satir, family therapist and writer, defined self-esteem as a feeling that "the person who I think I ought to be on the outside is the same as the person I know I am on the inside." If we have unrealistic expectations for who we ought to be, we'll never live up to our standards, and our self-esteem will suffer.

● **Put-downs are stressful.** Every put-down you accept—from yourself and others—erodes self-esteem. Negative self-talk, including name-calling ("You dummy! You klutz!") is like an acid that eats away at confidence and self-acceptance.

● **"Shoulds" can be subtle put-downs**, because you are constantly reminding yourself of what you have not done, rather than focusing on what you have done well. Imagine the benefits of giving yourself routine pats on the back instead of kicks in the behind.

● **You can change criticism to praise.** Focus on your positive attitudes. Practice describing your actions instead of judging them. Try saying, "I lost my keys" instead of " I'd lose my head if it wasn't fastened on."

13) The trainer invites participants to practice positive self-esteem.

➤ Turn to your partner and spend a minute affirming yourself.

➤ Talk for one minute, without stopping, about all your positive qualities, behaviors, and attributes.

➤ No criticism or put-downs are allowed. Make positive statements only.

☞ *To expand this focus on self-esteem, insert the **Self-Esteem Pyramid** (**Wellness 5**, p 15) here.*

D. Stress and Entitlement (15–20 min)

14) The trainer introduces the concept of entitlement and its relationship to stress and self-esteem.

● **Lack of entitlement is stressful to many women.** Entitlement refers to our willingness and ability to claim personal rights, feel worthwhile, and take action on our own behalf. Women traditionally have been socialized to do the exact opposite: to deny their rights (or give them away!), find fault with themselves, and defer to the needs of others.

● **Entitlement is a belief that grows from self-respect and self-worth.** If you love and respect yourself, you believe you deserve a quality life and are entitled to take actions to make this happen.

● **Take advantage of Superwoman status.** You can reduce stress by claiming your rights. Become your own sympathetic permission giver, and allow yourself to take control of your life without guilt or apology.

15) The trainer instructs group members to form groups of four based on the month of their mother's birthday.

➤ The person with the most sisters is appointed timekeeper.

➤ Each person has 2 minutes to talk about a responsibility you are carrying which is causing you stress.

➤ Listen attentively, without judgement or comment, when other women are speaking.

16) The trainer invites participants to share examples of these stressful responsibilities, and makes the point that women often suffer unnecessary burdens because they do not feel entitled to ask for help with these responsibilities, especially at home.

17) The trainer gives a copy of the **Bill of Rights** worksheet to each participant, and explains a process for identifying personal rights.

➤ Think again about the things you have been feeling guilty about, and the expectations and responsibilities you have been taking on yourself.

➤ Ask yourself:

➣ Are my expectations reasonable?

➣ What do I need to stop feeling guilty, raise my esteem, and reduce stress?

➣ What specific rights do I need to claim?

☞ *Stimulate ideas with examples: the right to have a career, rest, share work at home, etc.*

➤ List all of the rights you want to claim on the front of the podium on your **Bill of Rights** worksheet.

☞ *Allow 3–4 minutes for this portion.*

18) When group members have completed their **Bill of Rights**, the trainer gives instructions for affirming these rights.

➤ Look over your Bill of Rights and select one that is especially difficult for you to accept for yourself.

➤ Stand up in a circle with your group.

➤ The person to the right of the group reporter will go first.

➤ The first person should read your chosen right aloud to the group.

➣ Stand tall and use a strong, confident, convincing voice to declare your right.

➤ After the first person declares your right, other group members affirm that right by adding reasons which underscore the importance of acting on that right.

☞ *Demonstrate how this works: Person A says "I have the right to rest when I am tired." Person B responds, "You have the right to rest because you're human and all humans need rest." Person C adds a different reason, and so on until all group members have affirmed Person A's right.*

➤ When people are affirming your rights, listen quietly, accept their comments, and thank them for their support.

> When everyone has responded to the first person, the next person reads your right and receives affirmation for it.

> Go around the group until each of you has the opportunity to read your right and receive affirmations.

19) The trainer regathers the group and asks for examples of rights that were declared, reaffirming each right by restating it and writing it on newsprint.

E. Strategies for Change (10–15 min)

20) The trainer introduces yet another right to which all participants are entitled—the right to develop strategies for coping with stress. This serves as a bridge to the closing chalktalk and planning process.

● **Low esteem is a woman's stress.** If you work on raising your self-esteem, you will reduce your stress. Raise your self-esteem by refusing to put yourself down and by focusing on your positive qualities and accomplishments.

● **Awareness of your unique stress patterns is the first step toward changing them.** Notice the ways that the media bombards you with images and messages about how to be a Superwoman. Pay attention to your response to these messages. Learn to laugh at your own Superwoman fantasies.

● **Shared responsibility is a major stress for both married and single women.** Instead of apologizing for your need to share the work at home, develop a sense of entitlement, so that you can approach family members with confidence and conviction that you deserve a fair balance of responsibility.

● **Initiative is a key factor in reducing stress.** Don't wait to be rescued or for others to give you permission to change your life. Take charge, take action, be in control of life as much as possible. When you are in control of yourself (not others!), your stress level will go down, and your ability to cope will increase.

● **Support is essential.** Seek support where you need it—at home, at work, in your neighborhood, church, and community. People who have a strong support network cope with stress better and stay healthier when experiencing life crises. They are also less likely to see themselves as Superwomen.

● **Balance is the key**: work and play, self and other, solitude and social contact, challenge and acceptance, stress and relaxation. No one area of your life should dominate. Consider your physical, mental, social, spiritual, and relational needs.

● **Relaxation is the daily bread of stress management.** Practice relaxation, and become your own relaxation expert. Develop a personalized plan for daily unwinding. This might be hot baths, aerobic exercise, relaxation tapes, soothing music, meditation, saunas, novels, massage, or other methods. A psychologist once said, "If you're not practicing relaxation, you're practicing anxiety." Stop practicing anxiety and start practicing relaxation.

21) The trainer distributes **Stop Superwoman Stress** worksheets and presents its model for stopping Superwoman stress: Make your life **EASIER** with **B**alance and **S**upport.

➤ Look over the strategies outlined in the acronym **EASIER** with **B**alance and **S**upport.

➤ Reflect on your strengths and weaknesses in each of these eight dimensions of stress management.

➤ Mark with a star one or two areas where you would like to develop skills for making your life easier.

➤ Write down one or two ideas for actions you can take to develop these areas.

22) After participants have had the opportunity to write down some of their ideas for change, the trainer encourages group members to share their plans with their small group.

➤ Allow each person one minute to share their ideas for change.

VARIATIONS

■ Close the session by having participants complete an *Affirmation Calendar*, p 73.

■ The *Superman* energizer (p 126) makes a good companion to this exercise.

Chalktalk points in **Step 2** *are adapted from a speech on the* **Superwoman Syndrome** *given by columnist Ellen Goodman at the Westminster Town Forum, St. Paul MN, and broadcast on Minnesota Public Radio.*

SUPERWOMAN STRESS SYMPTOMS

RELATIONAL
• perfectionism • troubled relationships
• violence • resentment • trying to be "good"
• taking on more work • dependency • nonassertiveness
• lowered sex drive • nagging • conflicts
• clamming up • isolation • distrust • lack of intimacy
• using people • can't say "no" • all roles are important

SPIRITUAL
• feeling worthless • alienation • lack of support • no laughter or play
• apathy • loss of direction • needing to prove self • cynicism • guilt
• over-commitment • looking for magic • martyrdom • emptiness
• loss of meaning • victim mentality • values conflicts • spiritual neglect

PHYSICAL
• headache • colitis • appetite change • backache • cardiac arrhythmia
• asthma • allergies • neck pain • chronic fatigue • weight change
• chest pain • hyperventilation • cold hands/feet • use of alcohol/drugs
• increased smoking • foot-tapping, finger drumming • pounding heart
• amenorrhea • PMS • anorexia • bingeing • pale, sallow complexion
• digestive upsets • muscle spasm • dizziness
• tension • accident proneness • frequent illness
• insomnia • blood pressure changes

MENTAL
• indecisiveness • rigid thinking • poor concentration
• boredom • spacing out • lethargy
• forgetfulness
• erratic work performance
• feeling overwhelmed
• negative self-talk • dulled senses
• lack of creativity
• difficulty seeing alternatives
• procrastination

EMOTIONAL
• impatience • panic attacks • irritability • guilt-ridden
• instant anger • depression, the "blues" • anxiety
• crying spells • difficulty holding in feelings
• mood swings • feeling trapped
• nightmares • worrying
• easily discouraged
• lack of reliance

BILL OF RIGHTS

©1995 Whole Person Press 210 W Michigan Duluth MN 55802   (800) 247-6789

Make Your Life EASIER:

Esteem

Awareness

Shared Responsibility

Initiative

Entitlement

Relaxation

---

with

B A L A N C E

and

S U P P O R T

©1995 Whole Person Press 210 W Michigan Duluth MN 55802   (800) 247-6789

153 PICK YOUR BATTLES

This systematic procedure which helps participants target stressors that are important to change is especially useful when stress is overwhelming or it's difficult to decide when to start.

GOALS

To identify sources of stress.

To rank stressors in relation to their personal impact and potential for change.

To rank stressors in order of relevance or priority.

GROUP SIZE

Unlimited.

TIME FRAME

30 minutes

MATERIALS NEEDED

Stress Assessment worksheet for each participant.

PROCESS

1) The trainer starts with a short chalktalk on reasons that stress management attempts might fail or succeed.

   ● **Attempts to manage stress are often unsuccessful due to misdirected efforts.** We have a tendency to tackle the first problem we encounter or think of, rather than *picking our battles*. This haphazard approach often results in trying to change those things that are of little impact or importance, or trying to change those things that are highly resistant to change.

   ● **Seeing a threat in every situation** leads to endless battles against perceived dangers, and increases stress unnecessarily. If your habit is to look only on the negative side, it would be wise to develop more positive skills for relabeling situations as challenges and opportunities.

   ● **Picking your battles is the best strategy for managing stress.** The most effective approach is to tackle the stressors that have the most impact on our lives, those that are feasible to change, and those that present a genuine threat. This is the wisest use of our energy, and offers the greatest chance for success.

2) The trainer asks participants to form groups of 4–6 people, and then provides guidelines for small group discussions about the topic.

➤ Share examples with the group of times you picked the wrong battle.

➢ Choose times when you tried to change something unimportant to you or resistant to change, or a time when you fought an unnecessary battle because of a perceived threat when none existed.

➢ Be sure to note feelings of frustration and futility that complicated your stress response.

3) The trainer invites group members to share examples with the large group, emphasizing how these examples of misdirected efforts added to that person's stress level.

4) The trainer distributes **Stress Assessment** worksheets and invites participants to explore the most productive focus for their stress management efforts.

➤ Brainstorm a list of your current stresses.

➢ Write these stressors down the column on your worksheet labeled **stressors**.

➢ List them as they come to mind—do not put them in any order at this time.

    ☞ *Make sure everyone has a fairly long list before proceeding to the next step.*

➤ For each stressor, rate its **impact** or **importance**, using a 1 to 5 scale, ranging from low to high.

➢ You might consider how much the stressor bothers or inconveniences you, interferes with your work or relationships, or causes general distress.

    ☞ *For this and following steps, allow time for all to complete the task. Remind people there are no right answers. This is a subjective assessment.*

➤ Rate how feasible it is to change the stressor, or how much you can really influence it. Record the score in the column labeled **feasibility**, using the 1 to 5, low to high feasibility, scale.

➤ Decide how much real **threat** exists for each stressor, and rate it on the 1 to 5 scale from little to great threat.

> ➤ Be as objective as possible. Ask yourself, what is really at stake here? Am I overreacting or is there real danger?

> ☞ *Emphasize that problem solving based on only one of the criteria (i.e., impact, feasibility, or threat) is unlikely to be as successful as strategies that consider all three variables.*

➤ To determine the relative priority for each stressor, multiply the three ratings (impact, feasibility, and threat) and place the **product** under the column **Priority Score**.

> ➤ The stressor with the highest **Priority Score** is the most urgent stressor to you, based on its threat, its importance, and the likelihood of change being effected.

> ➤ Review the **Priority Scores** and rank all your stressors from highest to lowest priority, using the **Priority Rank** column.

5) The trainer responds to any questions participants may have about their stress assessments, and concludes by encouraging participants to focus their stress management efforts on those stressors with the highest priority scores.

VARIATIONS

■ Make separate stressor lists for different contexts of participants' lifestyle: work, family, relationships, health, financial, social, etc. Compare the Priority Scores of each context to see which deserve the most attention.

TRAINER'S NOTES

Submitted by David X Swenson.

©1995 Whole Person Press 210 W Michigan Duluth MN 55802   (800) 247-6789

PICK YOUR BATTLES

Priority Rank	Stressors	Impact 1 2 3 4 5	Feasibility 1 2 3 4 5	Threat 1 2 3 4 5	Priority Score

154 STORMY PASSAGES

In this open-ended stress assessment, participants visualize their reactions to a thunderstorm and apply their insight to the stormy passages of life.

GOALS

To identify stressful life situations and habitual coping patterns.

To activate emotional resources as motivators for insight and change.

GROUP SIZE

Unlimited.

TIME FRAME

20–30 minutes

MATERIALS NEEDED

Stormy Passages worksheets and blank paper (or journals) for all; **Stormy Passages** script.

PROCESS

1) The trainer introduces the storm metaphor for stress.

   ● **Storms are one of nature's most powerful forces.** We tend to think of them as destructive, but they also bring needed precipitation and bear on their winds the potential for pollination and rearrangement of the landscape.

   ● **The storm can also be seen as a metaphor for stress**—particularly major life stresses that threaten to overwhelm us with their intensity. Stormy periods are often times of crucial change and subsequent growth. The storms of our life, when we survive them, tend to strengthen and shape us.

2) The trainer distributes blank paper and invites participants to sit back, close their eyes and join in an intriguing visualization. The trainer reads the **Stormy Passages** script.

3) Before the mood of the imagery is broken, the trainer asks participants to respond to a series of questions about their experience during the visualization.

©1995 Whole Person Press 210 W Michigan Duluth MN 55802   (800) 247-6789

☞ *Give people plenty of time after each question to recall their moods and capture them in words.*

✔ Where were you at the beginning of the image and how did you feel when the skies were clear and sunny?

✔ How did you feel when the storm started to gather on the horizon? A bit anxious? Unmoved? Expectant? Intimidated?

✔ How did you feel as the storm approached closer and closer? Apprehensive? Exhilarated? Disappointed?

✔ How did you feel when to storm broke over you, in the midst of the ferocious squall? Powerful? Helpless? Scared? Energized?

✔ How did you feel as the intensity diminished and the storm began to move off? Relieved? Disappointed? Anxious? Did the stress leave slowly or quickly?

✔ How did you feel when the storm had disappeared and all was calm again? Energized? Relaxed? Let down?

✔ Did you move at all during this storm? Or take any action? If so, describe your movements.

✔ Finally, what was your favorite part of this image: sunshine before the storm, the storm on the horizon, the storm approaching closer, the midst of the storm, the storm letting up, the storm disappearing, or the calm after the storm?

✔ And your least favorite part?

4) The trainer asks participants to pair up with a partner and gives instructions.

➤ Decide who is *lightning* and who is *thunder*.

➤ *Thunders*, begin by describing your feelings during the visualization and telling your favorite and least favorite parts.

➤ After two minutes you will switch roles, and *lightnings* will describe their feelings during the storm and identify favorite and least favorite parts.

☞ *Keep time and notify after two minutes.*

5) The trainer distributes **Stormy Passages** worksheets and invites participants to reflect on the stressful storms in their own lives.

➤ Think about the stress of your life. Imagine these stresses as storms of various types, lengths, and intensity.

➤ Some may be immediate minor squalls such as a clash with your teenager, an overdue project, or a balky battery in your car. Or you

©1995 Whole Person Press 210 W Michigan Duluth MN 55802   (800) 247-6789

              may be experiencing a major, extended upheaval like divorce, the death of someone close to you, or corporate reorganization.

       ➤ Consider stress related to your health, your family, your lifestyle, changes in your life, or other personal issues.

       ➤ Don't forget about stress at work and in the wider environment of your community and world.

   ➤ Identify several of these stress storms in your life and locate them on the worksheet. Put as many stresses as you can into your picture.

       ➤ Use symbols or brief descriptions and locate them where they currently are in the storm sequence.

       ➤ Some stresses may be over and done with, almost out of sight. Put them off to the side where the clouds have passed by.

       ➤ Others you may be right in the midst of, with thunder and lightning all around. Identify these current storms.

       ➤ Some are probably looming on the far horizon, approaching slowly or quickly. Find an appropriate place to locate these impending storms.

         ☞ *Allow plenty of time for people to generate their stress picture. In necessary, stimulate thinking with examples drawn from your knowledge of the group. When most people have run out of steam, move on to the next step.*

6) The announcer challenges participants to call on their inherent creative capacity to make connections.

   ➤ What are the connections you see between the storm you visualized earlier and the stresses you included in your **Stormy Passages** worksheet?

   ➤ On the bottom or back of the worksheet jot down some of your feelings, insights, or discoveries.

7) When most have finished writing, the trainer invites participants to share their storms and insights with their partners.

   ➤ Take about 3 minutes each to show your worksheet and share your insights.

   ➤ *Lightnings* start first.

   ➤ *Thunders* are welcome to ask questions, but not give advice or make comparisons.

   ➤ Please be respectful of each other's privacy boundaries.

       ☞ *Keep time and signal when partners should switch roles.*

8) The trainer reconvenes the large group, invites comments, and uses theses responses to make a transition to an appropriate learning activity focused on effective stress management.

VARIATIONS

■ As a part of *Steps 6* and *7*, participants could choose one specific stress and describe it, in detail, to their partner, using the storm metaphor and elaborating on their feelings during the various stages of the stress storm.

This exercise was inspired by Lyman Coleman.

STORMY PASSAGES Script

Imagine you are somewhere outdoors . . .
on a summer day . . . on a golf course . . . in a canoe on a placid lake . . .
walking on the beach . . . sitting on a tractor in a prairie cornfield . . .
hiking in the mountains
somewhere outside where you can enjoy the expansive horizon . . .
the blue sky above punctuated be an occasional puff of clouds . . .
Notice how you are feeling as you relax in the pleasant calm of this view.

Now imagine that the sky begins to darken . . . the wind begins to pick up . . .
and big thunder clouds are gathering on the horizon . . .
Notice how you feel as you watch the distant threatening storm
beginning to approach closer and closer . . .
What do you do? How do you feel?

The temperature drops suddenly and the storm breaks over you . . .
it is a furious squall with high winds, thunder and lightning . . .
Notice where you are and how you feel . . .
in the midst of the storm's turmoil . . .

And now you begin to notice the storm's intensity abating . . .
the squall is moving on . . . the winds are dying . . .
Notice how you feel as the storm passes on . . .
Does it leave slowly or quickly?

And now, finally, the storm has disappeared over the horizon . . .
followed by clear skies and sunshine . . .
Notice the freshness the storm has left behind and notice how you feel
as you gaze out once again across the placid landscape.

STORMY PASSAGES

155 WINDOWS ON STRESS

In this adaptable, multilayered assessment participants use mental software to explore the interactive windows of their stress.

GOALS

To explore the multifaceted nature of stress.

To break down a complex life stress into more manageable components.

To identify stress that needs attention.

GROUP SIZE

Unlimited.

TIME FRAME

30–45 minutes

MATERIALS NEEDED

Windows on Stress worksheets; newsprint easel, marker board or overhead projector with transparencies; one Hi-lighter for each person (in four colors so members of small groups can trade for different steps).

PROCESS

1) The trainer begins with a chalktalk on stress, appropriate to the group and previous session content, incorporating some or all of the following points.

   ● **Stress is a complex issue.** The stresses facing the mythical cavefolk were clearcut survival issues, including the immediate need to escape from dangerous predators. Our modern day stress is rarely so clear— neither the threat, nor the potential consequences, nor the best alternative for action.

   ● **Some stressors are more complex than others.** The stress of going for a dental checkup can't compare with the death of the family dog. The stress of a traffic detour is minor compared to the stress of living with an alcoholic.

   ● **Major life stress** such as divorce, death, trauma, chronic disease, mid-life crisis, the loss of a job, or moving **can be overwhelming**, even immobilizing, if we imagine we can or must manage them immediately and effortlessly.

● For most complex life stressors, it helps to tackle them one bit at a time, using a variety of coping strategies.

2) The trainer distributes **Windows on Stress** worksheets and announces that this creative problem solving technique, borrowed from Matsumua Yasuo, president of Clover Management Research in Chiba City, Japan, will help participants consider a major stressor from many angles, looking for manageable pieces.

> ☞ *Demonstrate each step with an enlarged version of the worksheet on newsprint, marker board, or overhead projector. Choose one example (eg. job burnout) and follow it through.*

➤ In the center square (or pane) of the center square (or window) write down a major stressor in your life. (eg, career change, divorce, family conflict, difficult child, health concern, pregnancy, financial setback, etc.)

➤ Surround your stress with some of the related stresses that accompany, include, or are caused by your central stress.

> ➤ Put one related stress in each window pane, starting with A and ending with H.

> ➤ Just jot down a key word or phrase.

> > ☞ *Give your example and then allow enough time for all to finish before moving on. Remind people there are no right answers—this is a subjective assessment and whatever comes to mind will help them understand their stress better.*

3) The trainer invites participants to take a closer look at these surrounding stresses by creating a separate window for each.

➤ Transfer the stress from **Pane A** of your central window to the center pane of the window in the center of the bottom row of windows. The pane is also marked A.

➤ Do the same with **Stress B, C, D** and on to **H**, making each one the center pane of a whole new window.

➤ Now begin with **Window A**.

> ➤ Surround that stress with some of the related stresses that accompany, underlie, or are caused by **Stress A**.

> ➤ Write these stresses in the panes marked 1, 2, 3 to 8.

> ➤ Don't panic if you can't fill every pane—something else will probably come to you later and you can go back and fill it in.

➤ Use the same process to identify the stresses surrounding window **Pane B, C, D** to **H**.

☞ *Again, remind people to trust their internal wisdom in making connections. Someone will probably comment that the same stress pops up in different windows. Acknowledge that, of course, our stresses overlap, but encourage people to stretch for additional different components of the stress.*

4) After nearly everyone has all the windows filled, the trainer notes that participants have identified 73 sources of stress, including their original central stress and all the related windows.

5) The trainer distributes Hi-lighters and when all have one, instructs participants to form groups of four finding three other people who have Hi-lighters of different colors.

6) The trainer asks groups to find chairs together and introduce themselves, briefly sharing one of their 73 stresses.

7) After about 2–3 minutes the trainer interrupts and invites participants to take a closer look at their stress windows, using Hi-lighters to mark appropriate panes on their worksheet, in response to a series of questions.

☞ *Allow time between each question for people to choose and mark their responses.*

➤ First, look through your 73 stresses and decide which one or ones are **causing you the most distress** right now.

➤ Using the Hi-lighter you received, make a big ✗ in the panes containing these especially distressful issues.

➤ Make a key at the bottom of the worksheet. Write *most distressful* and then Hi-light the word.

➤ Pass your Hi-lighter one person to the right so everyone has a new color.

➤ Now, look through your 73 stressors again and decide which one or ones you are **managing pretty well right now**, those you are coping with successfully.

➤ Using the new color Hi-lighter, make a big **exclamation point** in the panes containing stress you are coping with successfully for the moment.

➤ Add to your color key at the bottom, writing *coping* and Hi-lighting the word.

➤ Once again, pass your Hi-lighter to the right, so everyone has a third color.

➤ This time, look through your 73 stresses and decide which ones **you can learn the most from**, which ones will stretch you.

➤ Using the new color Hi-lighter, make a big **plus sign** in the panes containing stresses that will promote personal growth.

➤ Again, add to your color key, writing *growth* and Hi-lighting the word.

➤ For the last round, pass your Hi-lighter to the right again to receive your fourth color.

➤ This time, look through your 73 stresses and locate one or two that you believe **someone in your group** of four might be able to **help** you with.

➤ Using the fourth color, Hi-light **around the four sides** of that pane.

➤ Then add the word *help* to your color key and Hi-light it.

8) The trainer gives instructions for the final step of the assessment.

➤ Study the whole picture presented by your stress windows, looking for new perspectives and insights.

➤ As you notice surprises or connections or holes, or whatever you notice, write each insight down.

➤ Use the format: *I notice that . . .*

➤ Write as many insights as occur to you, but be sure to write at least five statements.

9) When participants have captured their insights, the trainer invites them to share their discoveries in the small groups. (15–20 minutes)

➤ Each person take about 5 minutes to show your **Stress Windows** patterns, and share your insights.

➤ Be sure to identify the stress you thought the group could help you with, and ask for that assistance.

➤ The person who has worked with computers the longest should start first.

☞ *Keep time and announce every 4–5 minutes that the spotlight should shift one person to the left. As groups are sharing, wander around collecting Hi-lighters and eavesdropping a bit.*

10) The trainer gathers the large group together and asks for comments, including potential applications for the **Windows on Stress** process.

☞ *Follow up this assessment with a presentation of stress management skills such as **Stress Management Alphabet**, p 58. Ask participants to match appropriate ABECEFG copers with the stresses they have identified.*

VARIATIONS

■ Adapt the questions in *Step 7* to the setting, audience, and course objectives. Questions that might be pertinent substitutes: *Mark the stresses that . . .*

> *you can't do anything about;*
> *you can't control;*
> *will probably take care of themselves without effort on your part;*
> *need immediate attention;*
> *would make a good starting place;*
> *where you've invested most of your energy;*
> *are a piece of cake to manage;*
> *you've been avoiding;*
> *conflict most sharply with your values/ethics;*
> *you need the most help with;*
> *you feel most hopeful about;*
> *you feel most hopeless about.*

■ To add a coping focus to this process, give people a second **Windows on Stress** worksheet after *Step 8*. Participants transfer the key stresses they would like to work on to the center panes of windows A to H, then surround each stress with potential coping strategies. In *Step 9*, participants share this worksheet and ask other group members for additional coping ideas. Participants use Hi-lighters to mark copers they will incorporate into a stress management plan.

■ For an amazing demonstration of the power of positive thinking, repeat the exercise through the first part of *Step 3*, transferring the eight stresses from the center window to the center panes of the outside window, Then using each stressor as a focus, identify eight surrounding **positive elements** of that stress or issue. See *Silver Linings*, p 55 for an expansion of this optimistic idea.

■ This is a superb tool for exploring health concerns, feelings, or career options (eg, Personal qualities I could bring to a job; or Desirable aspects of a perfect job).

*The techniques used in the **Stress Windows** worksheet originated with Yasuo Matsumura, president of Clover Management Research in Chiba City, Japan. We first read about it in James H Higgins' wonderful book, **101 Creative Problem Solving Techniques** (Winter Park FL: The New Management Publishing Company, 1994).*

WINDOWS ON STRESS

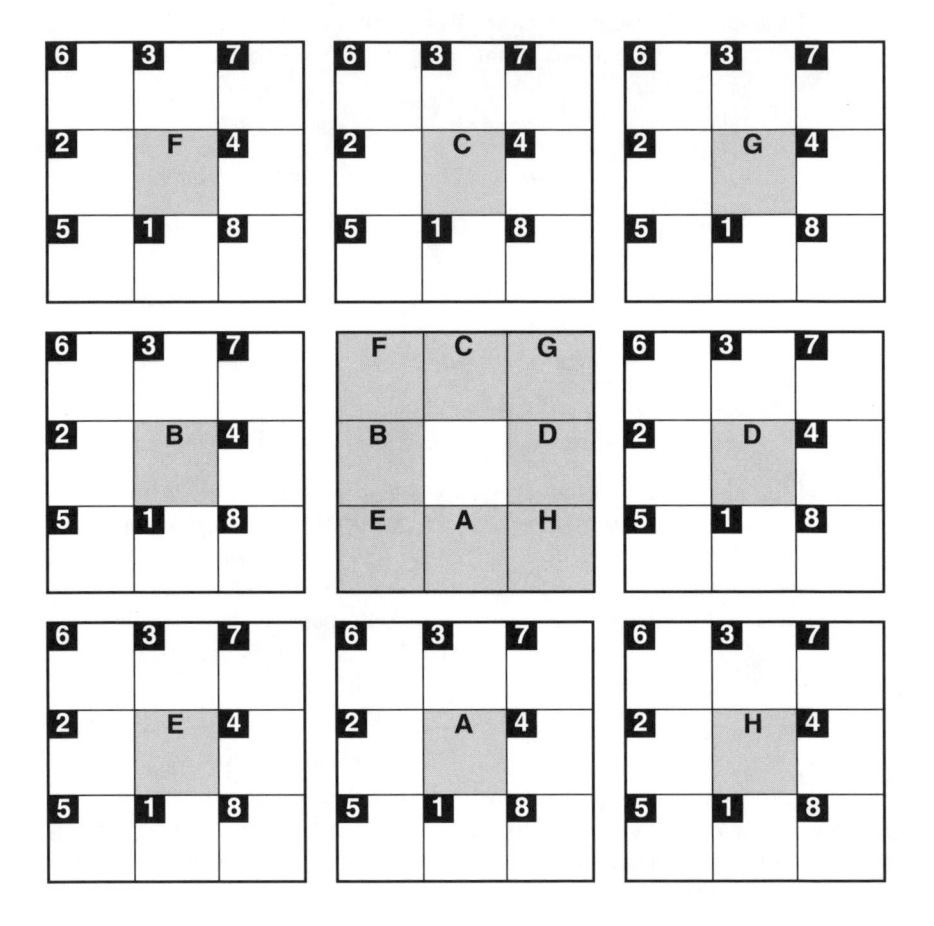

Management
Strategies

156 MANAGING JOB STRESS

This thought-provoking short video and self-analysis process gives participants the tools they need to identify, analyze, and plan strategies for coping with on-the-job stress.

GOALS

To recognize the variety and intensity of work-related stresses.

To learn new skills and ways of coping with "hot spots" that cause job stress.

GROUP SIZE

Unlimited.

TIME FRAME

20–60 minutes

MATERIALS NEEDED

A VHS VCR and monitor; the videotape *Handling Workplace Pressure*, first of six in a series on **Managing Job Stress**, available from Whole Person Associates, 210 W Michigan St, Duluth, MN 55802. 1-800-247-6768. FAX 218-727-0505. (Purchase cost $95.00, includes Leader Guide and five Skill Building Guides for participants. Additional Skill Building Guides, which include additional content material, intriguing worksheets, process instructions, and summaries of the videotapes, are available at an attractive discount.)

PROCESS

☞ *This 20–minute video can be used alone for a quick presentation, or incorporated into a longer reflection and sharing process as described here. Maximum benefit comes with the balance of all three in a one-hour session: 20 minutes of video, 20 minutes of reflection, 20 minutes of sharing.*

1) The trainer provides a warm-up chalktalk on the universal nature of job stress, and invites participants to reflect on their current job stress using the **Pressure Cooker** worksheet.

2) The trainer asks participants to introduce themselves to each other and briefly describe their pressure cookers.

©1995 Whole Person Press 210 W Michigan Duluth MN 55802   (000) 017 0700

3) The trainer plays the videotape.

☞ *This 20–minute video asks a variety of people—experts and every-day folks—what's stressful about their jobs. There are a variety of answers—balancing work and motherhood, changes in workload, deadlines, etc. The video also includes a three-minute closing relaxation sequence.*

4) The trainer guides participants through a reflection process about job stress affecting them, and then invites them to share their observations in pairs.

5) Participants explore five areas of work-related stress: expectations, work-load, relationships, change, and balance, using an **On the Job Stress Grid**.

6) The trainer reviews the **Take Five** quick skills for managing stress: Take a breath, Take stock of stress-creating habits, Take action, Take it as it is, and Take care of yourself. Participants apply these skills to stressful work situations.

7) Participants identify situations or patterns they want to alter and share their stress managements goals with other group members.

TRAINER'S NOTES

*Based on the **Managing Job Stress** video series (Duluth MN: Whole Person Press, 1994).*

©1995 Whole Person Press 210 W Michigan Duluth MN 55802   (800) 247-6789

157 QUESTIONABLE COPERS

Participants analyze their negative coping patterns and explore healthier alternatives.

GOALS

To identify questionable coping strategies and typical stressful situations where they are used.

To track occurrences of negative coping behaviors and substitute more positive strategies.

GROUP SIZE

Unlimited.

TIME FRAME

30–40 minutes

MATERIALS NEEDED

Questionable Copers Log worksheets; newsprint and marker.

PROCESS

1) The trainer begins with a definition of questionable copers.

   ● Coping methods which offer immediate tension relief but have short or long-term negative consequences are questionable strategies for managing stress on a regular basis.

2) The trainer asks the group for examples of such negative or questionable copers and writes these on newsprint.

   ☞ *Prompt the group, if necessary, with examples: smoking, alcohol, withdrawal, etc.*

3) The trainer further explains the cost of negative copers in a chalktalk.

   ● **Questionable copers have undesirable side effects.** Getting sick, feeling depressed, or taking out your frustrations out on the family are all ways of dealing with too much or too little stress. Overwork, overeating, alcohol, drugs and smoking are common escape routes. Unfortunately, the side effects of these copers usually outweigh the benefit of temporary relief from stress.

● **Negative copers are temporary solutions.** While some coping styles give immediate relief, they don't last very long and they can't be continued over a very long time. Throwing a temper tantrum may be effective occasionally, but who wants to pout all the time? A little white lie may get you out of a tense moment but is likely to come back to haunt you. A hot fudge sundae or a shopping spree can be terrific for your morale—but both have long range consequences.

● **Negative copers are stress producing.** Short term tension relievers like lighting up a cigarette, kicking the dog, cutting a class, or mentally checking out usually create more problems than they solve, especially if they're repeated often. We call these short-term remedies with high pricetags *negative copers*.

● **Minimize questionable copers.** All coping patterns, negative and positive, work—or we wouldn't do them. Denial reduces short-term stress by removing a source of worry from your mind. Yet denial carries the risk of ignoring important signals that your well-being is at stake. To manage stress effectively, it is important to minimize your use of negative, high-risk copers.

3) The trainer distributes **Questionable Copers** worksheets and reads the list, giving explanations for each negative coper.

4) The trainer guides participants through their self-assessment, so that they are completing this process step-by-step as they go along.

➤ In **Column A**, add other negative copers you might be tempted to use from the group list or your private list.

➤ In **Column B**, indicate how frequently you use each negative coper. Circle R = Rarely, S = Sometimes, O = Often.

➤ In **Column C** list the types of stressful situations in which you typically use each coper.

➤ Write the benefits/rewards you gain from using the coper in **Column D** and the costs/drawbacks of the coper in **Column E**.

5) The trainer asks everyone to choose a questionable coper from the list for a personal focus, and directs participants to form small groups of 4–6 people by joining with 3 or 4 others who share that interest.

6) Once groups have gathered, the trainer gives instructions for discussion.

➤ Each person identify three negative copers you would most like to stop using, and describe them to your group.

> ➤ When everyone has identified your personal top three, brainstorm together healthier coping strategies that could replace each questionable coper.

5) The trainer reconvenes the large group, asks for examples, and builds a list of healthier alternatives, writing them on newsprint, and asking participants to take notes on all ideas.

> ☞ *You may need to expand the group's ideas with some of these: chewing gum, stretch break, focused breathing, brisk walk, talking it out, music, writing, warm bath, working with your hands, Yoga, exercise, nap, physical labor, reading, sex, gardening, deep relaxation, prayer, meditation, blowing off steam, play, entertainment.*

6) The trainer asks participants to choose 2 alternative behaviors for each of their top 3 questionable copers and write them in **Column F** on their worksheet.

7) The trainer challenges participants to keep a log during the next week (or whatever time period they want), noting every time they are tempted to use a questionable coper in **Column G**, and recording every time they use a healthier alternative in **Column H**.

TRAINER'S NOTES

The list of questionable copers is taken from **PILEUP**, *a colorful stress management card game available from Whole Person Press, Duluth MN.*

QUESTIONABLE COPERS LOG

A. Questionable Coper	B.	C. Stress situations when I use it	D. Benefits/ Rewards	E. Costs/ Drawbacks	F. Alternatives	G. Questionable	H. Alternative
						FREQUENCY	
Smoking	R S O						
Alcohol	R S O						
Eating	R S O						
Tantrums	R S O						
Passivity	R S O						
Indulging myself	R S O						
Revenge	R S O						
Fault finding	R S O						
Worrying	R S O						
Denial	R S O						
Illness	R S O						
Stubbornness	R S O						
Drugs	R S O						
	R S O						
	R S O						
	R S O						

158 SILVER LININGS

In this thoughtful exercise, participants discover silver linings in a problem-cloud, and use these ribbons of light as inspiration for coping strategies.

GOALS

To discover opportunities for growth inherent in a problem.

To develop strategies for handling a troublesome dilemma.

GROUP SIZE

Unlimited.

TIME FRAME

20–30 minutes

MATERIALS NEEDED

Blank sheet of paper for each participant.

PROCESS

1) The trainer begins the exercise with a brief chalktalk about the way that problems can be transformed into possibilities for growth.

   ● **"Pain is a part of life and an opportunity for growth."** This statement by the late Virginia Satir, pioneer in family systems theory, summarizes her human growth model of therapy. Based on the concept of discovering potential for positive change in troublesome situations, family conflicts can be transformed into opportunities for dialogue and intimacy.

   ● **When you are stuck, take a second look.** Finding new ways out of a dilemma takes time and effort. In the words of C.W. Metcalf, "In this life, pain and misery are free; laughter, joy, humor—the elements that make life worthwhile—take a little effort."

   ● **Consider the health benefits of changing negatives to positives.** We know that the stress response is activated by negative thoughts and perceptions of danger and alarm. If you identify growth opportunities in a worrisome situation, you are going to be less anxious. Positive thinking combined with positive actions will interrupt the stress response and help you to relax and cope more effectively.

2) The trainer distributes blank sheets of paper to each participant, informs them that they will now have the opportunity to practice these ideas, and proceeds to guide them through the steps of the process.

➤ Close your eyes for a moment and think about a problem that is causing you stress and worry.

➢ Focus on all of the negative aspects of this problem; think of all the reasons why this problem causes you pain and misery.

➤ Open your eyes and draw a picture of a cloud which symbolizes your problem.

➢ Embellish your drawing with shading, lightning, rain, wind, or any other element that depicts your feelings when you think about this problem.

➢ Write any negative words that describe the unpleasantness of this problem.

➤ Now put yourself in the picture. Draw yourself somewhere on the page, showing the effect of this problem on your mood and outlook.

☞ *Allow 4–5 minutes for this portion of the exercise.*

3) When participants have finished drawing their clouds, the trainer gives directions for a second drawing.

➤ Turn your paper over.

➤ Keeping this same problem in mind, draw a new cloud to represent it in a different way.

➢ This time think about all the possible benefits and opportunities for growth that are hidden within your cloud.

➢ Draw in silver linings for each of these opportunities, and label them with a few words or adjectives to describe the potential joys and possibilities for growth.

☞ *If participants seem stuck, challenge them to think of the benefits of their problems. Give them permission to be outrageous or humorous. Possible benefits could be: mental challenges, reminders to respect their feelings, deepening of faith, clarification of values, new friends, or greater intimacy with people who share the problem.*

➢ Embellish your drawing with sunlight, shadows, wind, or any elements you think depict the way that your cloud could be transformed by these silver linings.

➤ Now put yourself in the picture somewhere, showing the effect that finding silver linings in your cloud can have on your mood and outlook.

4) After participants have finished their second drawing, the trainer guides them through a final reflection and planning process.

> ➤ Study both of your drawings.

>> ➤ How could you use the opportunities presented by your silver linings to cope with your problem?

> ➤ Incorporate these insights into an action plan for coping with this problem.

>> ➤ How might you grow in the process?

>> ➤ Write your plan somewhere on your silver linings drawing.

5) When everyone has recorded insights and made a plan, the trainer invites participants to share any inspirations that they may have discovered in their silver lining drawings.

6) The trainer concludes with a brief chalktalk.

- **Personal growth often follows a hard time or traumatic event.** Common examples include family members growing closer at a time of death or crisis, deepening of faith after a trauma, and discovery of new meaning after a serious illness.

- **Possibilities for growth exist in small, everyday problems.** To take advantage of these opportunities, you need to keep an open mind and take the time to look for positives. This requires a letting go of anger about a problem (Why me? What did I do to deserve this?) and a willingness to move on and make the best of the situation.

- **The skills of relabeling are enduring.** If you continue to practice, you will give yourself a positive outlook which will help you cope with stress at every stage of life.

TRAINER'S NOTES

159 STRESS MANAGEMENT ALPHABET

This widely acclaimed prescription for stress management is as simple as ABC, fun to do, and exciting to learn.

GOALS

To learn a new paradigm for managing stress

To apply stress management strategies to personal life situations.

GROUP SIZE

Unlimited.

TIME FRAME

50–60 minutes

MATERIALS NEEDED

Blackboard or newsprint; microphone for groups over 20, a horn or harmonica for trainer's use; and **Stress Management Alphabet** worksheet.

PROCESS

☞ *This process assumes that participants have previously explored their current stressors and coping styles through an exercise like* ***Stress Windows****, p 43.*

1) The trainer begins with reference to prior learning about stress and coping, noting that everyone in the room has a personal prescription or formula for how to manage stress. Participants are invited to compare notes on coping styles.

   ➤ Find a partner.

   ➤ Take a minute to tell each other your formula for managing stress.

2) The trainer blows a harmonica to regain attention, then invites participants to share examples of their prescriptions with the group.

   ☞ *Be sure to affirm volunteers for their good ideas.*

3) The trainer distributes **Stress Management Alphabet** worksheets and outlines the alphabet prescription for coping with stress: **A**ttitude, **B**alance, **C**ommitment, **D**o, **E**xaggeration, and **F**ocus.

4) The trainer introduces the first skill, **Attitude**, and leads participants through completion of the attitude section of the worksheet.

©1995 Whole Person Press 210 W Michigan Duluth MN 55802   (800) 247-6789

● **A is for Attitude.** People who live long, healthy lives have a positive outlook on their lives and responsibilities. Where others may find problems and disappointment, good stress managers see challenge and opportunity. They find humor in difficult situations, laugh at themselves, and cultivate feelings of gratitude. These attitudes promote healthy responses to stress and create more options for coping.

➤ Turn to the first section on your worksheet, labeled **attitude**.

➤ Think of one *stressor* in your current life and write it in the appropriate space.

➤ Now reflect on your attitude toward the stressor.

➢ In the second space record how your view this stressor.

➢ Jot down all the things you say to yourself about the situation (eg, "This is hopeless, we'll probably never make it!").

➤ Now ask yourself: Is there another way for me to look at this?

➢ In the third space jot down alternate ways of looking at the same situation (eg, "We could ask for extra help," or, " I always learn from my mistakes.").

➢ Don't judge whether your alternatives are practical or realistic. Give yourself permission to develop a new point of view.

➤ Now consider other healthy attitudes you could develop around this issue.

➢ Jot down your ideas in the last attitude space.

5) The trainer introduces the second skill of **Balance** by leading the group through an exercise to demonstrate the concept, giving a brief chalktalk, and then guiding the group in further reflection using their worksheets.

➤ Please stand up.

➤ Alternate touching your right hand to your left knee and your left hand to your right knee.

➤ Continue doing this for 1 minute.

☞ *Point out that by doing this exercise, participants are achieving balance between the right and left brain, and now they need to consider how to get the rest of themselves balanced.*

● **B is for Balance.** Our body, mind, and spirit move naturally toward balance. Unfortunately we sometimes get in the way. We pick at a sore that's healing, push ourselves when our body's yelling "rest!" and struggle for answers that our spirit already knows if we would just calm down and listen.

● Listening to ourselves is the key to finding balance. Your shoulders will tell you if your carrying too heavy a load. Or your stomach will say "Too much coffee, I'm upset!" The answers to our need for balance lie within us.

➤ Notice some area of tension in you body and pay attention to it.

   ➢ What is your body telling you?

   ➢ What about your mind and spirit?

➤ Now look at how you spend your **time** and see if it feels balanced for you. Fill in the second section of your worksheet, labeled **Balance**.

   ➢ How much of your energy is directed toward body, mind, and spirit?

   ➢ How much is for work, play, relaxation?

   ➢ How much for self, family, friends?

➤ Make notes about any discoveries or decisions you made about balance in your life.

    ☞ *Encourage participants to process their discoveries and any issues which came up.*

6) The trainer summarizes the skill of **Commitment** in a chalktalk, and leads participants through the next step of their worksheet.

● **C is for Commitment.** Without a true commitment to your heart, mind, and body, all the other stress management techniques won't make a difference. A commitment requires you to say, "Yes—I am ready. I do care about my well-being and I will do something about it." It also means saying "yes" to people and events that contribute to your well-being and "no" to those that add unhappiness to your life. Commitment also means surrender, letting go of something. You can't say "yes" to something without letting go of something else. Yes to marriage means letting go of single life, yes to parenting means certain limits on career and social life.

➤ Turn your attention to the third section of your worksheet and reflect on your commitments.

➤ List your current commitments. What are you now saying "Yes" to?

   ➢ How committed are you to each? 80%, 90%, 100%?

   ➢ Are there additional commitments you want to make? Add these to your list.

➤ Have you included yourself in your commitments? What commitments would you like to make to yourself?

➤ Add these commitments to yourself.

➤ What will you need to say "No" to?

7) The trainer invites participants to commit themselves to more involvement with each other by joining in a group backrub.

    ☞ *Make sure that participation is consensual and not forced. Give
permission for anyone who does not want to participate to say
"No," and relax on the sidelines.*

➤ Stand up and form a circle, with each person facing the back of the
person in front of you.

➤ Put your hands on the shoulders of the person in front of you, give
a back and shoulder rub for one minute.

➤ Then turn around, face the other direction and give the person in
front of you a back rub.

    ☞ *Point out that now that everyone is relaxed and revitalized,
it's time to move on to* **D—Do.**

8) The trainer summarizes the fourth skill of **Do** in a chalktalk, demonstrates this skill with a physical activity and short visualization, and helps
participants apply this skill to their lives by completing the next
worksheet section.

● **D is for Do.** Stop thinking and do something. Your body knows when
you need to move, run, walk. Your mind and body crave variety.
When you are under stress, do something different! We get in ruts
doing the same old thing about the same old problems. Be quiet and
still in order to listen to your internal voice of wisdom. If something
feels right, trust yourself and do it!

    ☞ *Ask participants if they are tired of sitting and suggest a short
stretching exercise.*

➤ Stand up. Now stretch your arms way above your head.

➤ Groan a little.

➤ Now stand with your feet apart at shoulders width, allow your upper
trunk to relax and your lower trunk to feel firmly planted on the
ground. Get your heels down on the ground.

➤ Now relax your mind and imagine you're facing a beautiful scene ten
feet in front of you.

➤ Now with your palms facing backwards at your side, swing your arms
back as far as they'll go and let them naturally swing forward. Now
back and forward. Keep doing it.

☞ *Congratulate participants on doing something to get their oxygen flowing and get their body more relaxed and revitalized. Then direct the group to **Section D** on their worksheet and guide them leisurely through the reflection process.*

➤ What could you do right now—or at the next break, or end of the session—that would feel good for you, and be out of the ordinary?

➤ Ask yourself: What feels right for me at this time of my life? Now is the right time for me to do what differently?

➤ List other things you could do differently to revive your energy and your outlook.

➤ Share one of your ideas with someone nearby.

9) The fifth skill, **Exaggeration,** is explained with a chalktalk and demonstration before participants complete their worksheet.

● **E is for Exaggeration.** Exaggerating a physical sensation or an emotional feeling helps you let it go. When you exaggerate your physical tension you pay attention to it, you increase it, and your natural response is to let go. You notice the difference between tension and relaxation and you choose the more pleasant state. The same is true emotionally. When we exaggerate our dilemmas and struggles, we see how serious we have become—and can then let go and laugh at ourselves. Laughter is healing and helps us to see more clearly what is important to us.

➤ Focus on a spot in your body that's tense.

➤ Increase that tension, hold it, exaggerate it for 15 seconds or more—and then let it go.

➤ Repeat one more time.

✔ Feel better?

➤ Now stand, move around, and greet other participants by exaggerating your handshake, pumping up and down vigorously.

☞ *Tell participants that now that they've had a chance to exaggerate their tension and feelings, they can look at the positive role of exaggeration in stress management.*

➤ In the *exaggerate* section of your worksheet, write down one way that you use exaggeration right now in you life.

➤ Then list some additional ways you might exaggerate and "carry on" to relieve tension and promote more laughter in your life.

➤ Share an exaggeration idea with one of your neighbors.

☞ *Solicit ideas from the group about how they could exaggerate to relieve tension and record these on newsprint.*

10) The trainer describes the final skill, **Focus**, in a chalktalk and guides participants through further reflection about the current focus of their lives.

   ● **F is for Focus.** You become what you focus on. If you're focused on positives, you'll find happiness and contentment. If you're focused on negatives, you'll find frustration and dissatisfaction. Focus on something you can do something about. This will give you back personal power you gave away trying to control others. Focus on *your* feelings, *your* attitudes, and *your* actions. Focus on the here and now. Live the moment and enjoy the gift of today.

   ➤ Reflect upon the current focus of your life.

      ➣ What are you focused on at this time in your life?

      ➣ Jot down your responses in the *focus* section of your worksheet.

   ➤ Are there other healthier places to focus?

      ➣ List these and enjoy them.

11) The trainer encourages participants to make a commitment to themselves today to care for themselves, live life enjoyably, and practice these A-B-Cs, predicting that if they do, they will be even spunkier and more contented then they are now. All it takes is:

   A for Attitude.
   B for Balance.
   C for Commitment.
   D for Do.
   E for Exaggerate.
   F for Focus.

12) The trainer recommends that participants turn their worksheet over, take a minute and write their own prescription for how they will make their A-B-Cs work.

VARIATIONS

■ This would be an excellent follow-up to *Windows on Stress,* p 43.

Submitted by Mary O'Brien Sippel.

STRESS ASSESSMENT ALPHABET

ATTITUDE
Stressor:
How I see it:
Another way to look at it:
Other attitudes to develop:

BALANCE
Body/mind/spirit:
Work/play/relaxation:
Self/family/friends:

COMMITMENT
Current commitments:
Commitment to myself:

DO
Do something out of the ordinary:
Do differently at this time of my life:
Other things I could do differently:

EXAGGERATE
One way I use exaggeration now:
Exaggerate more in my life:

FOCUS
My current focus:
An even healthier focus:

©1995 Whole Person Press 210 W Michigan Duluth MN 55802   (800) 247-6789

160 YESTERDAY, TODAY, TOMORROW

In this empowering exercise, participants assess the amount of time they mentally spend in the past, present, and future, and are encouraged to capitalize on the power of the present moment.

GOALS

To understand how being present to ourselves keeps us well.

To learn practical ideas for staying in the present moment.

GROUP SIZE

Unlimited.

TIME FRAME

20–30 minutes

MATERIALS NEEDED

Yesterday, Today, and Tomorrow worksheets.

PROCESS

1) The trainer ask participants to estimate the percentage of time they spend focused on **the past** (memories, guilt, sadness, resentment, regrets, fears, and embarrassment about past events), **the present** (here and now activities and interactions), and **the future** (worries, anxieties, apprehensions, and dreams about future events). The total must add to 100%.

2) The trainer polls the group by a show of hands to see what percentage of participants spend the most time in the past, present, or future.

3) The trainer invites participants to pair up with a neighbor to introduce themselves and compare notes on their involvement in past, present, and future.

4) The trainer invites examples of being out of the present moment and weaves these responses into a chalktalk about stress and worry.

   ● **Worrying about the past or future is unproductive.** Experts have estimated that 30% of our psycho-physical stress reactions are caused by past worries. Reliving the past causes us to re-experience these feelings in the present. Only 8% of the things we worry about for the future are legitimate. About 50% of dreaded future events never happen, another 12% couldn't be controlled anyway.

● **There are two days in every week that should be free of worry, fear, and apprehension.** One of these is yesterday, which is now beyond our control. We can't go back, relive the day, or undo our actions. The second worry-free day is tomorrow, with all of its challenges, burdens, promises, and threats. Tomorrow is also beyond our immediate control.

● **Today is where we should focus our energy and attention.** We have one moment of power, and that is now. Preoccupation with the past and future robs us of the power of the present moment. Reliving past glories or dreaming about the future can also be stressful. If our head is in the clouds, we're likely to miss what's happening in the here and now.

5) The trainer distributes copies of the **Yesterday, Today, and Tomorrow** worksheet and gives instructions for completing it.

➤ Make a list of all the past, present, and future things you're concerned about.

➤ In the **left column**, list things from **the past** that continue to be on your mind in the present—delightful memories as well as less happy memories of mistakes, regrets, or painful incidents that you tend to dwell on.

➤ In the **right column**, list aspects of **the future** that occupy your time and energy in the present—heroic dreams as well as concerns, anxieties, and worries.

➤ In the **middle column**, write down things that truly need your attention **today**.

6) When everyone has completed a list, the trainer directs participants to place a large "X" through their **yesterday** and **tomorrow** columns, indicating that the stressors for today are the ones they should focus upon.

7) Group members are invited to spend a few minutes thinking about positive actions they can take **today** to deal with these stressors.

➤ In the bottom portion of your worksheet, list things you can do today to handle today's stress.

☞ *Ask for an example of today stress and give ideas for managing it (eg, tackle one part of the problem, exercise, stop and relax, etc).*

©1995 Whole Person Press 210 W Michigan Duluth MN 55802   (800) 247-6789

8) The trainer solicits ideas from participants about the kinds of things they discovered they could do today. She weaves these suggestions into a chalktalk giving practical tips for staying in the present.

- **Always arrive three minutes early.** This will give you some time to breathe, relax, shift gears, and clear your mind for the next agenda.

- **When you find yourself wandering around in your mind, bring yourself back to the present.** Think of words or images that could help you bring yourself back to the here and now. For example, say "Now," take a deep breath, and imagine yourself alert and attentive. Or focus on the physical presence of the person you are with.

- **If you are a compulsive worrier**, practice confining your anxiety attacks to a specific, limited time period or location, such as a favorite chair. Try surrendering your concerns to your spiritual source or to the fates.

- **Practice being in the present.** Plan empty time and don't fill it! Learn to flow with time. Stop scaring yourself with the future or past. Substitute calming thought or activities in the present (gardening, jigsaw puzzles, reading inspirational poems, affirmations, walks).

- **Choose to alter your lifestyle to allow yourself your time.** Build in time for exercise and daily relaxation. Take care of yourself physically, emotionally, mentally, and spiritually. By being present to yourself, you will be able to be present to others.

- **Make conscious choices about how you spend your time.** Don't give away all your time or energy trying to please others or gain approval. Consider what is the most productive use of your time today.

VARIATIONS

■ At the end of the exercise, participants work in small groups to develop strategies for dealing with their favorite (most persistent) worries about the past and future.

YESTERDAY, TODAY, AND TOMORROW

Yesterday	Today	Tomorrow

_____   _____
_____   _____
_____   _____
_____   _____
_____   _____
_____   _____
_____   _____

©1995 Whole Person Press 210 W Michigan Duluth MN 55802   (900) 017 0700

TRAINER'S NOTES

Skill Builders

161 AFFIRMATION CALENDAR

Participants fill a calendar with rich, positive statements about themselves, and read these thoughts for daily affirmations in the coming month.

GOALS

To affirm positive attitudes and behaviors.

To practice affirmation as a stress management skill.

GROUP SIZE

Unlimited.

TIME FRAME

25–30 minutes

MATERIALS NEEDED

Whole Person Affirmation List, Affirmation Calendar and ten small (3x5) notecards for each participant.

PROCESS

1) The trainer introduces the topic with a short chalktalk about the power of affirmation in stress management.

   ● **Self-esteem is a powerful dynamic in both creating and relieving stress.** Self-affirmation is a powerful stress management skill. The more positively we view ourselves and our capabilities, the less likely we are to perceive life events as threatening, and the more resilient and resourceful we can be in facing life's challenges.

   ● **An affirmation is a strong, positive statement** about something that is already true. It is short, simple, and unqualified. It is in the present tense rather than in the past or future because it is already so. Negative words are not included. "I accept and love myself" and "I am calm in a crisis" are examples of affirmations.

   ● **Affirmations reinforce positive attitudes and behaviors.** Affirm means to make firm, give shape, substance, and permanence. Affirmation involves wanting a change, believing change is possible, and accepting the change when it takes place.

   ● **People with positive mental outlooks experience the greatest success** in education and career achievement, personal relationships, and overall health. Optimists are more resistant to illness and disease, make a quicker recovery, and live longer than pessimists.

● **Daily affirmations are a way to reprogram or replace stressful negative self-statements.** They are also reminders to stop judging and doubting yourself, and to stay focused on what your are doing well.

● **Affirmations can be silent, spoken aloud, written down, or chanted.** The method is not as important as the frequency. Affirmations should be repeated throughout the day.

2) The trainer announces that each person will develop a personal affirmation calendar. As a preparation for this exercise, the trainer hands out ten 3x5 notecards to each participant, and explains a process for getting started.

➤ On the first card write down ten things that you like about yourself.

> Be sure to include something you like about your mind, body, spirit, and relationships.

> Put a star by any affirmations that you would not have included five years ago.

3) The trainer asks participants to divide into small groups of 4–6 people by finding others who share their taste in music.

☞ *Prompt with suggestions of favorite musical categories (eg classical, jazz, rock, country, folk, gospel, rap, blues, etc). Designate areas for each group to convene. If groups are too large, advise people to form a second group.*

4) When everyone has joined a group, the trainer leads participants through a process of introductions.

☞ *Pause at each step until most groups are finished, but don't dawdle.*

➤ Introduce yourself to the group, read the list of ten things you like about yourself, and mention which ones you would not have included five years ago.

➤ When everyone has read your list, go around the group again and tell the group about one affirmation that you hope will be on your list five years from now.

➤ Write an affirmation for each person in your group on a 3x5 card, sign your name, and give it to the appropriate person.

> Affirmations should be short, simple, positive, rich with feeling, and in the present tense.

5) The trainer distributes a **Whole Person Affirmation List** and an **Affirmation Calendar** to participants and gives instructions for how to complete their affirmation calendar.

➤ Create a different affirmation for every day of the month and write them in your calendar.

➤ Use your list of likeable qualities to start.

➤ Write each affirmation in the present tense using simple positive statements with no disclaimers.

➤ Make sure you have a balance of affirmations for physical, emotional, relationship, mental, and spiritual self-care.

➤ Refer to the **Whole Person Affirmation List** for more ideas.

6) When everyone has completed their calendars, the trainer encourages participants to share their affirmations with their small group.

➤ The person who finished first is appointed timekeeper.

➤ Share your **Affirmation Calendar** with the group by describing some of your favorite affirmations.

➤ Each person has one minute to share.

7) After 5–6 minutes the trainer interrupts with a few tips for successfully using affirmations to manage stress.

● Keep revising your affirmation slightly as you encounter your internal resistance in the form of negative responses. When the affirmation rings true for you, repeat it fifteen times to get it firmly in mind.

● Keep repeating your affirmation, even when negative responses pop up. Write it down ten times or a hundred times. Sing it, Shout it. Whisper it.

● Imagine your life as if the affirmation has become reality. Then live your life as if it **is** reality.

8) The trainer closes the session by suggesting that group members hang their calendars in a prominent place in their home or office, and practice their affirmations often throughout each day of the month.

VARIATIONS

■ Group members brainstorm their own list of affirmations, which individuals then use as a resource.

Submitted by David X. Swenson, who credits Wally Johnston with composing the list of affirmations.

©1995 Whole Person Press 210 W Michigan Duluth MN 55802   (800) 247-6789

WHOLE PERSON AFFIRMATION LIST

PHYSICAL

I enjoy sensual pleasures • I rest when I am tired • I am strong and healthy • I am healing old wounds • I nourish myself • I love and care for my body • I play and have fun • I pace myself • I relax and slow down • I accept and affirm my sexuality • I choose to be healthy • I exercise regularly • I care for myself when I am sick • I am getting better every day

RELATIONAL

I say "no" when I want to • I can ask for help when I need it • I am trustworthy • I can ask for what I want • I allow others the right to be wrong • I affirm others • I accept affirmations from others and thank them • I handle conflict and tension with confidence • I share hugs with people • I am a loyal and committed person • I seek out people who love and nurture me

MENTAL

I put my worries in perspective • I accept reality • I can close my eyes and relax at will • I learn from my mistakes • I am worthwhile • I am a friend to myself • I choose what I want and go after it • I accomplish my goals • I am open-minded • I keep a positive attitude • I live in the present moment • I plan for my future • I encourage myself • I look for solutions • I am centered and balanced • I can change • I am creative

SPIRITUAL

I am joyful and peaceful • I grow and change • I am true to myself • I pray • I forgive myself • I am following God's plan • I am a creature of God • I am in harmony with the higher power • I have faith and hope • I let go of resentment • I value myself • I focus on beauty • I nurture my spirit • I respond positively to life • I welcome each new day • I am a part of everybody • I am kind and compassionate • I act on my beliefs

EMOTIONAL

I give up my jealousy • I express my feeling respectfully • I love myself • I express my individuality • I accept my feelings as a natural part of myself • I enjoy laughter • I am gentle with myself • I choose that which I enjoy • I listen to my feelings • I accept responsibility for my life • I take action when something is important to me • I cope with stress well

©1995 Whole Person Press 210 W Michigan Duluth MN 55802   (800) 247-6789

AFFIRMATION CALENDAR

SUNDAY	MONDAY	TUESDAY	WEDNESDAY	THURSDAY	FRIDAY	SATURDAY

©1995 Whole Person Press 210 W Michigan Duluth MN 55802   (800) 247-6789

162 EATING UNDER STRESS

Participants examine their patterns of eating, drinking, and smoking under stress, and develop strategies for modifying problem behaviors.

GOALS

To identify personal patterns of eating, drinking, or smoking under stress.

To learn more positive strategies for managing these stress symptoms.

GROUP SIZE

Unlimited.

TIME FRAME

40-45 minutes

MATERIALS

A blank sheet of paper and an **Eating Under Stress** worksheet for each participant; newsprint and markers for each small group; masking tape.

PROCESS

1) The trainer distributes a blank sheet of paper to each participant, and invites them to reflect upon their personal connections between stress and eating.

   ➤ Write three statements which describe your pattern of eating, drinking, and smoking under stress.

2) The trainer asks participants to share their responses with another group member.

   ➤ Pair up with a person you do not know well.

   ➤ Read your three statements and briefly explain them to your partner.

3) The trainer reconvenes the group, distributes copies of the **Eating Under Stress** worksheet, and combines a chalktalk on stress and eating with a process of personal reflection by participants.

   ● **Stress alters eating patterns.** When we're under stress, the who, what, where, when, why, and how we eat may change dramatically. The nature of the changes will be different for each person because people respond to stress differently. This applies to eating habits as well as other habits. Everyone has a unique pattern, based on cultural, social, religious, and economic factors.

● **WHAT. Stress can change what you eat and drink.** For some folks, stress takes away the appetite. Others binge on junk food under pressure. Stress can zap energy needed for planning, shopping for, and cooking nutritious meals. When you're overwhelmed and tired, who can resist convenience foods—or fast food joints with playgrounds for the kids? Stress can trigger cravings that may be insatiable.

> ➤ In what ways does being under stress affect **what** you eat and drink? Record your responses in the *What?* row of your worksheet, under the column labeled *Effects*.

● **WHO. Stress can determine your eating companions and your reactions to them.** Relationships may be disrupted, schedules upset, routines changed. A deadline at work may tempt you into a series of candy bar lunches with co-workers. Travel schedules may leave you eating suppers with children—or alone. Sometimes the people we eat with can cause us even more stress—such as holiday meals with relatives or important business dinners.

> ➤ In what ways does being under stress affect the **who** dimension of your eating, drinking, and smoking patterns? Record your ideas.

● **WHERE. Stress can change where we eat.** At times of high stress you may eat in the car, at your desk, or standing in the kitchen. A parent is critically ill and you eat all your meals in a hospital cafeteria. Your kitchen is being remodeled and you eat your meals in the family room—or in restaurants.

> ➤ How does stress affect **where** you eat, drink or smoke?

● **WHEN. Stress can change when you eat or drink**. Stress often disrupts our natural rhythm and regular schedule, leading to erratic eating patterns. You may work so hard you tune out your body and forget to eat lunch. Stress may cause insomnia, leading to midnight refrigerator raids or an alcoholic nightcap. If you're agitated and tense, stress can keep you snacking or smoking all day long.

> ➤ In what ways does stress affect **when** you indulge your oral satisfactions?

● **WHY. Stress can change why you eat.** Under stress we may find ourselves imbibing as a universal response to all kinds of needs. Instead of eating because you're hungry, you might eat, drink, or smoke for tension release, comfort, companionship, or security. Instead of eating or drinking to nourish yourself, you might self-medicate: a quick sugar fix from an ice cream cone, a cup of caffeine to keep you going, a glass of wine to help you sleep.

> ➤ In what ways does stress affect your **reasons** for eating, drinking, or smoking?

● **HOW. Stress can change how you eat.** Stress often creates a chronic sense of urgency. There's no time to relax. You have to hurry. You gobble your food, skip meals, or eat on the run. Or you might pick at your food, too preoccupied or worried to enjoy the meal. You may guzzle a beer or Diet Coke—or chain smoke.

> ➤ In what ways does being under stress affect the pattern of **how** you eat, drink, or smoke?

4) The trainer divides the group into six teams by having participants count off using the six questions: what? who? where? when? why? and how?

☞ *Depending on the total number of participants, you may have from 2 to 16 people in a group. Don't worry, any size will work fine. Assign meeting locations for each group, and as participants are gathering, distribute newsprint and markers.*

5) When teams are settled, the trainer gives instructions for exploring possible problem effects of stress..

> ➤ Brainstorm a list of possible problem eating, smoking, and drinking behaviors for your assigned question. (eg, the ***What?*** team makes a list of problem food or beverage choices, the ***Who?*** team lists relationship scenarios affecting eating under stress, etc).

> ➤ The person who most recently ate at McDonalds should be team recorder. Write down all ideas on your team newsprint.

> ➤ You have 5 minutes to complete your lists.

6) When five minutes have passed, the trainer interrupts and changes the focus with a short chalktalk about skills for managing stress.

● **Problem eating is a symptom of stress,** and not a cause. When we talk about skills for managing problem eating/drinking/smoking under stress, we are talking about symptom management. It is important to treat symptoms, but remember to do something about the underlying cause of your stress, if possible.

● **Skills are needed to manage stress.** Eating under stress is a complex issue and requires diverse stress management skills like planning, relaxation, tuning into your body, scouting needed resources, asserting your needs, flexibility, exercise, self-esteem, etc—and practical strategies like eating more often, but eating smaller amounts.

©1995 Whole Person Press 210 W Michigan Duluth MN 55802   (800) 247-6789

7) The trainer challenges teams to identify skills that might help someone manage the problematic eating/drinking/smoking under stress symptoms they have listed. (5 min)

> Use your collective wisdom to suggest skills and strategies a person might use to modify each of the problem eating/drinking/smoking examples your team listed on the newsprint.

> Record these coping skills and strategies on a new newsprint.

8) After five minutes, the trainer interrupts and asks team reporters to share their findings with the large group and post their newsprints. Participants are encouraged to identify potentially helpful skills for themselves.

> Beginning with the *What?* team, reporters describe 5 problem areas and 5 skills listed by your team.

> Everyone listen to the ideas presented, and reflect on which skills you might use to modify your own unique patterns of eating under stress.

> Take notes on your worksheet in the column marked *Skills*.

9) The trainer reconvenes the group and leads participants in further reflection and planning.

> Take out your original description of your eating under stress patterns.

> Write three new statements, summarizing your resolutions for changing one or more of these patterns.

10) The trainer concludes with a chalktalk summarizing the usefulness of this paradigm and reminding folks to attend to the causes of their stress.

● **Use this paradigm when you are under stress.** The What? Who? Where? When? Why? How? questions will help you get a handle on the dynamics of your symptoms, and how you can modify them.

● **Remember to address the source of your stress**, not just the symptoms. Both are worthy of your attention.

VARIATIONS

■ This paradigm can be adapted for examining any stress symptom or problem behavior: anxiety, depression, overwork, anger/temper problems, etc.

■ The process for **Eating Under Stress** is a perfect accompaniment for *Questionable Copers,* p 51. Apply the paradigm questions to each negative coper for a thorough exploration of these problem copers.

©1995 Whole Person Press 210 W Michigan Duluth MN 55802 (800) 247-6789

EATING UNDER STRESS

VARIABLES	EFFECTS		SKILLS
What? In what ways does stress affect what you eat and drink?			
Who? In what ways do people influence your eating/drinking/smoking?			
Where? In what ways does stress affect where you eat/drink/smoke?			
When? How does stress affect the frequency and timing of your eating/drinking/smoking?			
Why? In what ways does stress affect your motivations for eating/drinking/smoking?			
How? In what ways does stress affect your style of eating/drinking/smoking?			

163 KEEP YOUR COOL

This action-oriented exercise allows participants to practice skills for managing anger in provocative situations.

GOALS

To identify positive and negative effects of anger.

To minimize the negative effects of anger and maximize the positive effects.

To develop alternative strategies for dealing with angry feelings.

GROUP SIZE

Unlimited, as long as there is space for the concentric circles role play in *Step 12*.

TIME FRAME

60–90 minutes (with **Variation**)

MATERIALS NEEDED

One copy of the **Anger Control Panel** worksheet for each participant; large newsprint and marker; horn or whistle for trainer.

PROCESS

☞ *This exercise incorporates at least six potentially anger-provoking scenarios for role playing in* **Step 12**. *Prepare these in advance, tailoring them to fit your audience and setting (eg, stubborn two-year old in the grocery store, a colleague who didn't get a report done on time, waiting at the dentist, shoddy service in a restaurant, an act of injustice, striking out in softball, etc). Write the key elements of each scenario on a separate newsprint so participants will be able to read them easily.*

A. Anger: Feeling and Response (15–20 min)

1) The trainer introduces the topic by explaining that anger is a universal human emotion that everyone experiences. As a warm-up she asks participants to brainstorm a list of triggers for their anger.

   ✔ What are some of the things that make you angry?

   ☞ *Write ideas generated by the group on a newsprint labelled* **TRIGGERS**. *If necessary, prompt the group with examples: (eg, others being late, backseat drivers, children not doing chores,* *criticisms about your appearance, etc) Encourage people to think of examples from several areas of life: work, family, friends, recreation, health.*

2) When a long list of triggers has been generated, the trainer posts it where all can see and makes the distinction between **anger** and our **responses** to it.

● **Anger is a feeling**, an emotion we sense deeply inside. Our **response** to anger is exhibited in **behaviors** such as yelling, pushing, joking, leaving the scene, working harder, throwing a tantrum, problem solving, or many others. The **feeling** and the **response** are two different things.

3) The trainer begins a new list for **RESPONSES** to anger, and invites participants to brainstorm.

✔ How do you typically respond when you are angry?

✔ What are the behaviors you choose to manage your anger? Remember, these are the observable actions you take when you are angry.

☞ *Generate as many responses as possible. If participants seem to be holding back, urge them in a playful way to be honest. Ask how many serve cold shoulder for dinner. And what about sulking and pouting?*

4) The trainer weaves the responses of the group into a chalktalk on managing anger.

● **Anger is a totally natural and healthy feeling**. Our **responses** to anger, the way we act it out, and the way we manage it are not always so healthy.

● **Anger is an emotional reaction to certain kinds of provocative stress**. Emotional arousal produces physiological changes in our bodies: increased heart rate, tightened muscles, elevated blood-pressure, rapid breathing, and more. Emotions are invisible, but when they are aroused, some of our bodily reactions are observable: tears, red face, clenched teeth, shaking, bulging eyes, etc.

Behavior is an observable, external action taken in response to stimuli. Slamming the door, jogging, praying, cleaning the closet, shouting, throwing things are all behaviors we might choose in response to the stimulus of feeling angry .

● **Anger can have positive and negative effects.** Anger is an energizer. It arouses us physically and emotionally, stirring us up for action on our own behalf. Anger can stimulate us to resolve conflicts, express

©1995 Whole Person Press 210 W Michigan Duluth MN 55802   (800) 247-6789

and release tension, solve problems, confront injustice. Sometimes anger can help us feel in control and take charge of our lives.

This state of arousal has its negative side effects as well: stress on the body resulting from increased blood pressure, heart rate, blood sugar level, and muscle tension. Anger can provoke us to lose patience, act impulsively or become aggressive. This secondary behavior can then can disturb or harm work and personal relationships, causing even more stress.

● **The goal of anger management is to minimize its negative effects and maximize its positive effects.** Anger is most destructive when it is too frequent, too intense, lasts too long, is bottled up, leads to aggression, or disturbs work and personal relationships. Anger is most constructive when it is managed by staying cool and focused on problem-solving.

● **Managing anger in a healthy way takes skill**. In the **immediate situation**, we need skills to diffuse and evaluate: think before you speak or act, accept your part in the problem, exercise self control, empathize, show respect for yourself and others, and keep a problem-solving focus.

We also need anger management skills that will help us **prepare in advance** for handling provocative situations: awareness of your anger buttons, acceptance of yourself as human (all people get angry at times), willingness to be honest about what bugs you, ability to express your feelings assertively, and a variety of healthy ways to relax and release tension.

● **Anger management skills can be learned.** Don't lay blame for your temper on your fiery red hair or your feisty ancestors. You can decide to take control and be in charge of yourself. What you do with your anger—internally and externally—is up to you. Learn to make your anger work for you. Instead of bottling up or blowing up, keep your cool.

5) The trainer reiterates the three styles of managing anger and asks participants to identify examples of each style from the **RESPONSES** list generated earlier.

● Most people manage anger in one of three ways: bottling up, blowing up, or keeping their cool.

➤ Look over the list and find examples of blowing-up responses.

  ☞ *As the responses are identified, mark the examples on the* ***RESPONSES*** *poster using symbols:* ✗ *for blowup,* ✔ *for bottle-up, and* ○ *for keeping cool.*

➤ Go through the list again and identify bottle-up styles.

➤ Now find keeping-your-cool styles.

B. My Anger Pattern Worksheet (10–15 min)

6) The trainer distributes the **Anger Control Panel** worksheets and guides participants through an exploration of their personal style of anger management.

➤ Think about your typical style of managing anger.

➣ Do you bottle up, blow up, or keep yourself cool?

➣ Mark your typical response to anger in the *Anger Style Box* at the top right of the *Control Panel*.

➤ Now reflect on your *hot buttons*. What are some of the issues or situations that typically trigger your anger?

➣ Write one in each of the *Anger Buttons* on the left of the *Control Panel*.

➣ Refer back to the group list if you need ideas.

➣ Be very specific. What situations are likely to provoke your anger?

➤ Now imagine pushing one of these *Anger Buttons* and the effect it has on you.

➣ Draw a line connecting the trigger to the center circle, which represents *yourself* and *your internal perceptions*.

➣ In this circle, write down everything you can think of that goes on inside of you once your anger button is activated. Try to capture all aspects of your internal state of mind and body.

Your *feelings*, physiological responses (eg, tight chest, flushed cheeks).

Your *beliefs* about yourself and others (eg, Be strong, Don't cry, Mad is bad).

Your *history*, including your learned responses to anger (eg, Parents yelled, I yell).

Your *identity* and self-esteem. Who you are, how you are (eg, Help! I can't handle more criticism right now!).

Your *language*. What you say to yourself can be inflammatory (Like heck it can, fool!) or de-escalating (Stay cool).

Your *principles* and internalized rules about anger. (eg, Peace at any price, No hitting allowed).

©1995 Whole Person Press 210 W Michigan Duluth MN 55802   (800) 247-6789

7) When most people have identified the intrapersonal aspects of their anger, the trainer points out the connection between internal perception and anger management.

- Everything you included inside your circle is part of your anger experience, and will determine the meaning you attribute to the events listed in your anger buttons. This internal state of perception is a pivotal point for anger management, since we must decide what— if anything—to do about our state of arousal.

- The principles we internalize about managing anger are extremely important, because they serve as a compass for what direction we choose to follow when our dander is up: healthy, productive actions, or unhealthy, destructive behaviors, or some combination.

C. Eight Principles for Managing Anger (10–15 min)

8) The trainer continues with a chalktalk on the *Eight Principles for Healthy Anger Management*.

☞ *List these principles on newsprint as you go. Illustrate key points in your chalktalk with examples generated earlier by the group or from your own life experience.*

- **Just because you're aroused, you don't have to do anything.** Arousal—in this case anger—is a physiological response to certain stimuli. Arousal is a feeling state, not a license for action. Intense feelings can come and go in any given day, without our doing anything about them. For example, sexual arousal may occur without our acting on these impulses. Moods of fear or panic may hit us without our becoming hysterical or running away. We may feel euphoric or excited but stay calm. We may feel angry and choose not to do *anything*.

- **Choose to express your anger constructively.** Decide that you will make good things happen with your anger. Channel your energy into creative problem-solving, correcting an injustice, communicating honestly, and building closer, more satisfying relationships. Avoid indulging in destructive attitudes and behaviors like revenge, intimidation, control over others, martyrdom, self-righteousness, violence, shaming and blaming.

- **When aroused, stop and think.** Slow the process down. Give yourself time to evaluate the situation. What triggered your anger? Why? What other feelings besides anger do you have? Fear? Embarrassment? Disappointment? Hurt? What do you want from the other person, and from yourself? Can you be honest and direct about what you want? Mentally review your options. Think of at least six different alternatives.

● **Detach, don't escalate.** Escalation of anger is rarely helpful and often downright destructive. When we escalate, we intensify our feelings and are more likely to act on impulse. This is dangerous. Instead, cool down by taking an emotional step back from the other person or hot issue. Stop trying to control the other person or the outcome of the conflict. This does not mean giving up or withdrawing. It means assuming a *neutral* position in the heat of the moment.

● **Violence is not an option.** Unless this is truly a life or death situation, violence is not an appropriate way to deal with anger. Do no harm to yourself, others, your property, or pets.

● **Respect yourself and others.** Do not attack, blame, or shame others. Instead, respect the human rights and dignity of all people—including yourself. Accept the strengths and weaknesses of yourself and others. Acknowledge the subjective reality of others and allow different perceptions to be valid.

● **Assume responsibility for yourself.** When you own your feelings and take responsibility for yourself, you unhook from the trap of trying to control others. This is a key part of anger management, since efforts to control others will escalate anger and may cause harm. When you shift to an "I" position, you put yourself in the driver's seat by expending your efforts where it belongs: on controlling yourself.

● **Transform unconscious choices into positive actions.** Step out of the pathways of habit and try new, more helpful alternatives for managing anger. When you follow the eight principles for healthy anger management, you will increase your chances of enjoying the benefits of anger in your personal and professional life.

9) The trainer asks participants to consider how they want to handle their anger.

➤ Think about your positive choices for handling anger, once you are aroused.

  ➢ Try to apply the *Eight Principles for Healthy Anger Management* to the *Anger Button* you identified on your worksheet and the internal perceptions you recorded.

  ➢ Choose four or five different healthy actions you could take and write one in each box under *Behavior Choices*.

10) The trainer solicits examples of healthy behavior alternatives for handling anger, affirms these ideas, and reminds the group that their ability to

make these choices depends on how well they have exercised self-control at the moment of arousal.

● All of you in this room have the innate ability to control your own thoughts, feelings, and behavior.

● Look again at all of the forces at play inside your circle. This is where you need to focus your efforts to control the intensity of your feelings and thoughts before they lead to undesirable or unproductive behavior.

D. Anger Management Skills: Role Play/Application (20–30 min)

11) The trainer explains that while self-control is a critical skill for anger management, many other skills are also necessary. Participants are invited to brainstorm a list of additional skills for managing anger.

☞ *Write the skills on newsprint as they are suggested. Supplement as necessary (eg, owning feelings, listening, offering solutions, using "I" language, conveying respect, making eye contact, deep breathing, relaxation, time outs, empathy, validating the other person's perceptions, acknowledging feelings, saying what you want, and seeking more information). Label the list **SKILLS** and post it so all can see.*

12) The trainer briefly demonstrates several key skills from the list, then asks participants to pair up for practicing several anger management skills in a series of role plays.

☞ *Post the prepared scenarios where all can see them. Describe each scenario briefly.*

➤ Decide with your partner who will be **Rant**, and who will be **Rave**.

➤ Now make a large double circle with all the other pairs.

➣ **Rants** in the inside circle. **Raves** on the outside.

➣ Partners should be facing each other.

➤ **Rants** go first.

➣ Choose one of the provocative situations you would like to role play and tell your partner.

➣ Look over the list of skills for healthy anger management and choose one or two you would like to practice in this situation.

➤ **Raves** are to assume the role of provoker in the scenario.

➤ You will have one minute to play out the scene, with the **Raves** provoking and the **Rants** practicing their skills.

©1995 Whole Person Press 210 W Michigan Duluth MN 55802   (800) 247-6789

> ☞ *Clarify instructions if needed. Give the signal to start the role play, then blow your horn or whistle after one minute.*

➤ Stop now for one minute of feedback.

> ➣ **Rants** start by making one positive comment about your skill practice.

> ➣ Then **Raves** should give Rants positive feedback.

> ➣ Be sure to be concrete and specific. Restrict your comments to observations about behaviors and actions (eg, "You made good eye contact," "You had a calm tone of voice.")

> ☞ *Blow the horn after one minute and ask the **inside circle (Rants)** to move one person to the right for the next role play.*

➤ This time, with your new partner, **Raves** will choose the provocation to handle, and select a skill you want to work on.

➤ **Rants** act the role of provocateur.

> ☞ *Repeat this process of provocation, skill practice, positive feedback, and switching partner until everyone has practiced at least six times. Encourage participants to choose different scenarios and different skills for each role play.*

13) The trainer blows the horn a final time, announces that it is time for participants to sit down and stop ranting and raving.

14) After group members are settled down, the trainer asks them to pull out their **Anger Control Panel** one more time to review five steps for constructive anger management, summarized in the acronym **SAFER**.

● **S is for STOP. Stop and think.** Take a deep breath. Count to ten. Take a short time out. Do something physical like rake the yard or ride a bike. Think about what you are really angry about. Think about your anger buttons and the swirl of thoughts and feeling inside you. Do you need to act on them? How can you do this constructively?

● **A is for ACCEPT. Accept responsibility for your feelings.** Own your anger. Don't blame or judge others. Speak in the first person.

● **F is for FIND. Find alternatives to bottling up or blowing up.** Speak up. Use a conversational voice. Describe the situation that is bothering you in behavioral terms. Be specific. Adopt a problem-solving approach. Offer solutions. Find a humorous angle to the situation and laugh about it.

● **E is for EMPATHY. Empathize with the other person.** Look for the truth in their story. Listen for their feelings and acknowledge them. Validate their perceptions.

● **R is for RESPECT. Respond with respect**. Respect for yourself and others is the basic ground rule of anger management. It is not okay to shame, belittle, or attack, verbally or physically.

15) The trainer invites participants to apply these skills to their behavior choices.

➤ In the *SAFER* column at the right, write an action that you could take to manage your anger more productively, applying each of the five SAFER skills.

➣ In the first box, put an example of a *Stop and think behavior*.

➣ Write an example of *Accepting behavior* in the second box.

➣ Continue through the *F-E-R* skills.

16) The trainer solicits questions and comments from the group, and after responding to these, concludes the session by recommending that participants practice these skills and watch for positive results.

VARIATIONS

■ For a more thorough exploration of self-control in escalating or neutralizing anger arousal, incorporate *Remote Control*, p 91, as part of *Step 10*.

■ Expand this exercise by using *Pick Your Battles*, p 34, to help participants assess what's worth fighting about and when.

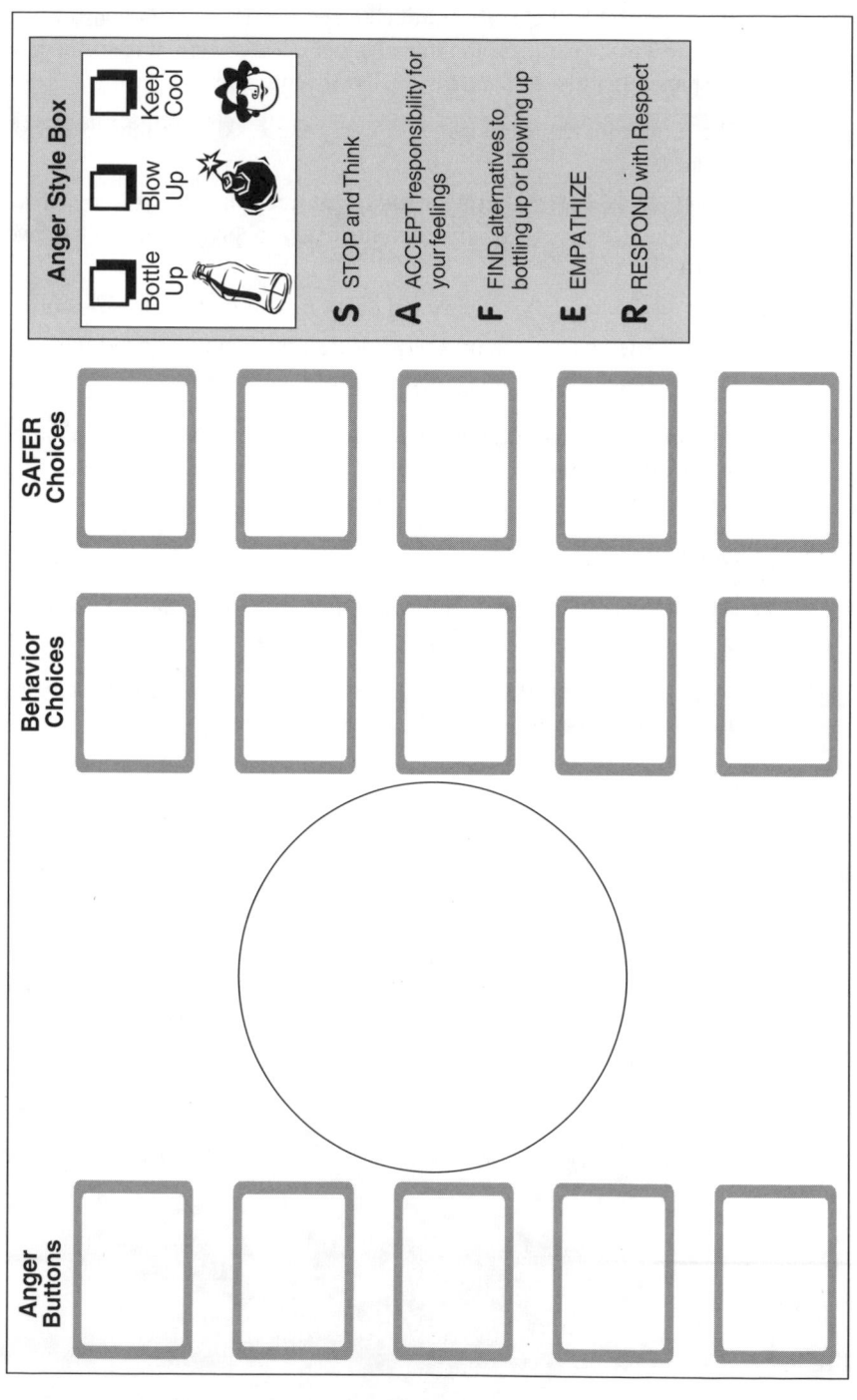

ANGER CONTROL PANEL

Anger Style Box

Bottle Up

Blow Up

Keep Cool

S STOP and Think

A ACCEPT responsibility for your feelings

F FIND alternatives to bottling up or blowing up

E EMPATHIZE

R RESPOND with Respect

SAFER Choices

Behavior Choices

Anger Buttons

164 REMOTE CONTROL

In this empowering exercise, participants draw upon innate, natural skills to change their mood and direct their behavior.

GOALS

To recognize that we can control our thought, feelings, and actions.

To reduce stress by actively changing our thought patterns.

GROUP SIZE

Unlimited. This exercise also works well with individuals.

TIME FRAME

20–30 minutes

PROCESS

1) The trainer conducts a quick survey by show of hands in response to a series of questions about times group members may have felt as if they were not in control of their lives.

   ✔ How many have felt like a victim of circumstances (eg, flat tire, traffic jam on the freeway)?

   ✔ How many have felt misled by another person or printed information?

   ✔ How many have felt "pushed to your limits" by others?

   ✔ How many have felt responsible for other people's feelings?

   ✔ How many have felt forced to do something you didn't want to do (eg, show up for work, undergo surgery, get up in the middle of the night to care for a sick child, etc)?

   ✔ How many have felt out of control in a particular mood, thought, or behavior (eg, anxiety, persistent worry, panic, anger, intense love or sexual desire, etc)?

2) The trainer introduces the concept of remote control.

   ● All people feel victimized and out of control of themselves at times, but, in fact, we are always in charge, operating with remote control in hand, processing information, reacting to it, and making choices about what chanels to explore.

3) To illustrate this point, the trainer asks everyone to stand for a quick demonstration.

➤ Raise your right arm up in the air.

➤ Let your left arm hang down by your side, and clench your fist.

➤ Now shout loudly "No—no—no—no—no!"

➤ Now jump out of the window.

> ☞ *People usually laugh when they get the point. Be prepared to intervene if someone actually tries to perform this stunt!*

4) The trainer observes that everyone followed the first three instructions, but nobody obeyed the last one and asks participants why they did not act on the direction to jump out of the window.

> ☞ *Participants will state the obvious: they did not want to hurt themselves.*

5) The trainer responds to group members' explanations with a chalktalk on the power of choice.

● **We always have choices**, even in dangerous situations. We can jump, not jump, argue, fight, run, be quiet, escape in fantasy, or a million other options. Victor Frankel, Jewish survivor of a World War II concentration camp, wrote that when all else is taken from us, we can still choose our attitude.

● **We do what we want to do**, within the limits of any given circumstance. We think what we want to think, believe what we want to believe, and choose the actions we want to take at any point in time.

● **A sense of control reduces stress.** When we own our feelings, thoughts and actions, we empower ourselves to feel a sense of control over our lives and are more able to cope with it, whatever comes our way. We all have the innate capacity to control our thoughts, moods, and behaviors.

6) The trainer announces that participants will now practice operating their remote controls to reduce distress about a difficult situation.

➤ Sit back in your chair, close your eyes, and turn your attention inward.

➤ Recall a situation that has been stressful or upsetting to you recently.

➤ Allow yourself to remember the vivid details of this unpleasant situation: where you were, who you were with, what was happening, and how you felt.

> ☞ *Pause long enough to for people to recall.*

➤ Now allow your unpleasant feelings to escalate, letting yourself become more anxious, frustrated, angry, or ashamed.

➤ Stay with these uncomfortable feelings for a moment . . . wallow in the feelings . . . let them get stronger and stronger.

☞ *Pause for 15–20 seconds.*

➤ Now reduce the intensity of these feelings. Turn down the frustration or anxiety knob so you feel a milder and milder version of what you felt before.

➣ Turn down your feeling internally, in whatever way you can.

☞ *Allow one minute of silence here for participants to mentally shift gears.*

➤ Still keeping your eyes closed, notice what you are telling yourself to lower the intensity of your feelings.

➣ Pay attention to any shift in your body posture, breathing, or other behavior changes.

➤ When you have noticed what you did to create milder feelings, open your eyes and return your attention to the room.

7) The trainer solicits feedback from group members about how the exercise went, asking by a show of hands how many people were able to change their feelings, and then inviting volunteers to share with the group what they did or said to themselves to increase and lower the intensity of their feelings.

8) The trainer records ideas on newsprint, and weaves these into a chalktalk summarizing the power or each person's internal remote control.

● **Use your remote control to reduce stress.** Turn down unpleasant thoughts, or turn them off altogether. Change the channel. Talk encouragingly to yourself. Think of positive steps you can take to solve a problem.

● **Use your remote control to increase your joy.** Just as you can escalate unpleasant feelings, you can also increase pleasurable ones. Recall a time of joy and celebration. Imagine places where you feel safe, relaxed, and peaceful. Affirm yourself.

● **Use your remote control to follow your heart**, and act in your own best interest. Listen to yourself, trust your instincts, and take actions in harmony with your values.

9) The trainer concludes by reassuring participants who could not change their mood to be persistent, practice the skill, and remember that they are exercising remote control with every choice they make.

The graphic demonstration in this exercise is courtesy of David Lamb, MSW.

165 YOGA

Participants experiment with basic breathing and posture techniques in this exploration of the stress management benefits of Yoga

GOALS

To explore the philosophy and techniques of Yoga.

To reduce tension and increase mental clarity.

GROUP SIZE

Unlimited as long as there is space for all to spread out comfortably on the floor.

TIME FRAME

30–60 minutes

MATERIALS NEEDED

Towel for each participant; if possible, provide exercise mats for all participants—at least make sure the floor has reasonably comfortable, clean carpeting.

PROCESS

☞ *Yoga is best taught by a certified instructor, but if you're not an expert, don't be afraid to introduce your groups to the basic concepts, breathing techniques, and postures. Many groups will have experienced Yoga practitioners in their midst. Why not ask for knowledgeable participants to aid in your demonstration and teaching.*

Gear the length and depth of your presentation to the interest level and physical flexibility of your audience.

1) The trainer begins by outlining the philosophy of Yoga and its health benefits.

   ● The philosophy and mind/mind/spirit techniques of Yoga originated in India thousands of years ago, and the basic principles were outlined by the sage Patamjali over 2,000 years ago.

   ● **Yoga is essentially a quest for spiritual realization** involving adherence to moral principles (non-violence, truthfulness, chastity, charity); purification of self through diet, self-discipline and study;

postures; breathing techniques; emptying of the mind through discon-
nection from inner and outer senses; deep concentration; meditation;
and the supreme state of the soul.

● Yoga practices are based on the philosophy that for a contented life,
you need a harmonious balance between your body, soul, and mind.
It's tough to maintain healthy equilibrium when we're under stress.

● The breathing techniques (*pranayama*) and postures (*asanas*) of
Yoga can be effective skills for stress management, even if you are not
interested in the ethical, dietary, or meditative components of the
philosophy.

● The easy stretching postures build strength and resiliency, increase
flexibility of joints and muscles, and promote physical and mental
resiliency. The mental attitudes and breathing routines of Yoga are
naturally calming and enhance concentration.

● **Yoga is a stress management techniques for all ages.** It's safe and
aesthetically pleasing to do. Research has demonstrated that practice
of Yoga can produce additional powerful health benefits such as:

> combatting stress and stress-related illness.
> lowering blood pressure.
> alleviating rheumatism and arthritis.
> reducing back problems.
> relieving migraine headaches.
> reducing fatigue.

2) The trainer invites participants to experience the relaxing effects of the
Yoga breathing technique called the **Complete Breath** of *pranayana*.

● **In Yoga the breath or *prana* is considered the life-force.** Yoga
believes that the more complete and rhythmic your breathing is, the
more life force you will have available.

● **The Complete Breath in Yoga is very slow and quiet.** Rhythm and
flow are most important. The Complete Breath happens in three
stages: abdomen, chest and shoulders. All breathing is done through
the nose.

➤ Sit as comfortably as possible, with your spine erect and your head
balanced.

➤ Place your feet solidly on the floor with legs slightly parted.

➤ Allow your palms to rest comfortably on your thighs.

➤ Start by tightening your abdomen muscles, noticing the control you
have over their expansion and contraction.

➤ Experiment with pushing your abdomen out as far as you can—and then contracting these muscles tighter, sucking in your gut.

➤ Practice these distensions and contractions a few times.

➤ Now begin a slow exhalation through your nose. Simultaneously contract your abdomen until your lungs are completely empty.

➤ Then begin a very slow inhalation and simultaneously push out your abdomen so the incoming air can get all the way to the bottom of your lungs.

➤ Continuing your slow inhalation, contract your abdomen slightly while you expand your chest as much as possible.

➤ Continuing to inhale slowly, raise your shoulders as high as possible, letting the air enter the very top area of your lungs.

➤ Hold on to your breath with your shoulders raised for a count of five: 1 – 2 – 3 – 4 –5.

➤ Now very slowly exhale.

➤ As the breath flows ever so slowly out through your nose, allow your body to relax.

➤ Contract your abdomen again at the end of the exhale, and without pause, repeat the breath.

➤ Inhale . . . belly out . . . chest out . . . shoulders up.

➤ Hold for a count of five: 1 – 2 – 3 – 4 –5.

➤ Slowly relax and exhale . . .

➤ Then contract your abdomen and repeat this breath three more times.

☞ *Remind folks to concentrate on allowing the movements to flow into each other.*

If there is time for more extended practice, include more Yoga breathing techniques here. Try the **Humming Breath** *(p 122) or exercises suggested in the* **Variations***.*

3) The trainer gives a brief introduction to the postures of Yoga and outlines three important guidelines.

● **Remember to keep breathing throughout**: Don't hold your breath—keep the flow going.

● **Pay attention to the feedback from your body.** Modify the pose so you can assume it with steadiness and ease.

● **Yoga is not a contest.** More is not better. Do not hold any posture longer than the recommended time. Be sure to stop if you feel any strain or shaking.

4) The trainer reminds participants to continue the complete breath technique as they assume the basic relaxation posture of Yoga called *Savasana*.

➤ Find a place to sit on the floor. Give yourself enough space around you so that you will be able to stretch out on your back later.

☞ *As participants are finding their spots, distribute folded towels. It helps if you start with everyone facing the same direction.*

➤ Remember to keep breathing in your flowing rhythm.

➤ Stretch your legs out in front to you and put your towel behind you, about where your head will be when you're fully stretched.

➤ Now lean back on your elbows, keeping your trunk and legs in line.

➤ Now lower your shoulders, head, and neck, adjusting the towel so your head is resting comfortably extended.

➤ Now stretch and extend your toes and legs, then let them relax. Allow your legs to roll naturally out to the side.

➤ Now stretch and extend your hands and arms, then let them relax comfortably at your sides, turning your palms up.

➤ Allow yourself to relax as much as possible in this posture for 5 minutes, focusing on the flow of your breath.

☞ *Remind the group to relax rather than to strain to achieve and hold this posture.*

5) After 5 minutes the trainer gently interrupts and invites participants to come out of their relaxation slowly.

➤ Imagine fresh energy entering every part of your body, starting at the head and moving down to the tips of your fingers and toes.

➤ When you are fully revitalized, slowly sit up.

6) The trainer notes that there are many Yoga postures and sequences that have different goals and benefits.

☞ *Demonstrate at least one additional posture, the Cobra (p 118). If time allows, try several from the list in the Variations.*

7) In closing, the trainer reviews the basic guidelines for using Yoga and encourages participants to seek additional training.

● Make sure your space for Yoga is quiet, warm, and free from distraction.

● Wear loose, comfortable clothes and make sure the floor surface is comfortable and not slippery.

● Practice regularly for 15–30 minutes a day.

● Always do Yoga on an empty stomach—just before a meal or two hours after eating.

● Take a break. Rest periods between groups of postures complement the beneficial effects of the stretches. Stop for 3–5 minutes and let the tension flow out and the vitality flow in with your breath.

● Find a qualified teacher and learn more about the various Yoga postures and sequences that have different goals and benefits.

● Stay loose!

VARIATIONS

■ To expand this presentation, demonstrate additional Yoga breathing techniques and postures from your own repertoire. Yoga techniques in other volumes of this series include: *Seaweed and Oak* (***Stress 2***, p 123), *Good Morning World* (***Wellness 2***, p 121), *As the Seasons Turn* (***Wellness 4***, p 116), *Cobra* (***Stress 5***, p 118). Breathing techniques based on Yoga include: *Cleansing Breath* (***Wellness 5***, p 116) and *Humming Breath* (***Stress 5***, p 122).

TRAINER'S NOTES

Planning
& Closure

166 FIVE AND TEN

In this quick assessment and planning process, participants focus on five stressors and a ten-step strategy for coping with one.

GOALS

To develop a plan of action to deal with a troublesome stressor.

GROUP SIZE

Unlimited. Works well with individuals.

TIME FRAME

10–15 minutes

MATERIALS NEEDED

One blank sheet of paper for each participant.

PROCESS

1) The trainer distributes blank sheets of paper to each participant and leads group members through a ten-step process for managing a difficult stressor in life.

   ➤ List five stressors in your life.

   ➤ Circle three that you want to work on right now.

   ➤ Underline two of those with which you have some idea of how to cope.

   ➤ Rewrite one of these, expanding it to include an example.

   ☞ *Give an example or two (eg, Arguments with kids might be expanded to include "Daily fights about homework and household chores with my two sons leave me frustrated, angry, and exhausted").*

   ➤ List five things that could be done to manage this stress.

   ➤ Circle two you can do.

   ➤ Underline one you want to try.

   ➤ Now consider what will hinder you.

   ➤ List three obstacles.

   ➤ What will help you?

➣ List three supports.

➤ Will you do it?

➣ Decide yes or no.

2) When everyone has completed the ten-step process, the trainer instructs participants to pair up with a neighbor and discuss strategies for dealing with their selected stressors.

3) The trainer invites volunteers to share their strategies for change, along with possible barriers and supports for these changes.

4) The trainer concludes the session by encouraging participants to follow-up on their plans for confronting their stressors, and recommends that they consider this ten-step method for dealing the other stressors they encounter in the future.

VARIATIONS

■ In *Step 2*, participants could share their five and ten plan with small groups from earlier in the learning.

■ This process could be adapted to fit different issues or interest groups. Instead of stressors, substitute other problems or topics: challenges, frustrations, conflicts, dreams, goals, areas of personal growth, etc.

TRAINER'S NOTES

167 GO FLY A KITE

In this uplifting ending to a learning experience, participants create a personal stress management program that is guaranteed to fly.

GOALS

To identify stressful feelings, attitudes, and behaviors as targets for change.

To reaffirm uplifting personal qualities and coping skills.

TIME FRAME

10–20 minutes

GROUP SIZE

Unlimited.

MATERIALS NEEDED

Go Fly a Kite worksheets.

PROCESS

☞ *The visualization* **Up, Up and Away** *(***Wellness 2**, *p 128) would make a nice mood-setting lead-in to this planning process.*

1) The trainer distributes **Go Fly a Kite** worksheets and introduces the kite as a metaphor for planning a stress management program.

   ● The stress of our lives often weighs us down, immobilizes us so we can't get off the ground, can't get moving towards needed change.

   ● The kite represents freedom. What steps do you need to take to be free from some of the stress that weighs you down or sends you into a tailspin?

   ● In order to lift us in times of stress, we need the strong winds of motivation as well as the stabilizing influence of our coping resources, support systems, and personal strengths.

2) The trainer asks participants to reflect on the stresses they have identified as problematic during the course of the learning experience and then guides the group through the worksheet to identify desired changes.

©1995 Whole Person Press 210 W Michigan Duluth MN 55802   (800) 247-6789

☞ *Pause long enough between questions for most people to write 3–5 items. Draw on previous discussions for pertinent examples from the group.*

➤ What stressful **attitudes** or **perceptions** do you need to drop in order to feel freer and less stressed?

➢ List these in *Section A* of your kite.

➤ What stress **behaviors** might you need to give up in order to feel freer?

➢ List these in *Section B* of your kite.

➤ What negative feelings are weighing you down (anger, guilt, fear, resentment, helplessness, etc)?

➢ List these in *Section C* of your kite.

➤ What **negative coping habits** keep you mired in your stress?

➢ List these persistent, stubborn parasites in *Section D* of your kite.

3) The trainer notes that focusing on stress is only the first step in stress management. Managing stress requires the best of our skills and personal resources. Participants are invited to identify some of their personal resources and motivation for lifting their spirits and reducing their stress.

➤ What are some of your personal qualities and coping skills that can help you manage your stress in a healthy manner?

➢ Since these are the stabilizing influence for you, write one skill or quality in each section of the kite's tail.

➤ No matter how many skills you have, your kite will never get off the ground without the wind—which represents your motivation for change. What are the motivators right now for you to change your patterns of responding to stress?

➢ Write each motivating factor in one of the wind arrows.

4) The trainer asks participants to summarize their resolutions for change.

➤ Write a one paragraph stress management program for yourself, using the image of your kite as a model for action.

➤ Include a statement of why this program is guaranteed to fly.

5) The trainer asks participants to rejoin previous small groups or pair up with a neighbor to read their paragraphs.

☞ *With fewer than 20 people, statements could be read to the entire group. Resist the temptation to drop this oral reading. Public affirmation of intended change is a powerful motivator.*

VARIATIONS

■ As part of *Step 3,* participants identify what core beliefs and values guide them in their life choices. These important elements, like the string of the kite, help keep us grounded. Write them on the string of the kite.

TRAINER'S NOTES

GO FLY A KITE

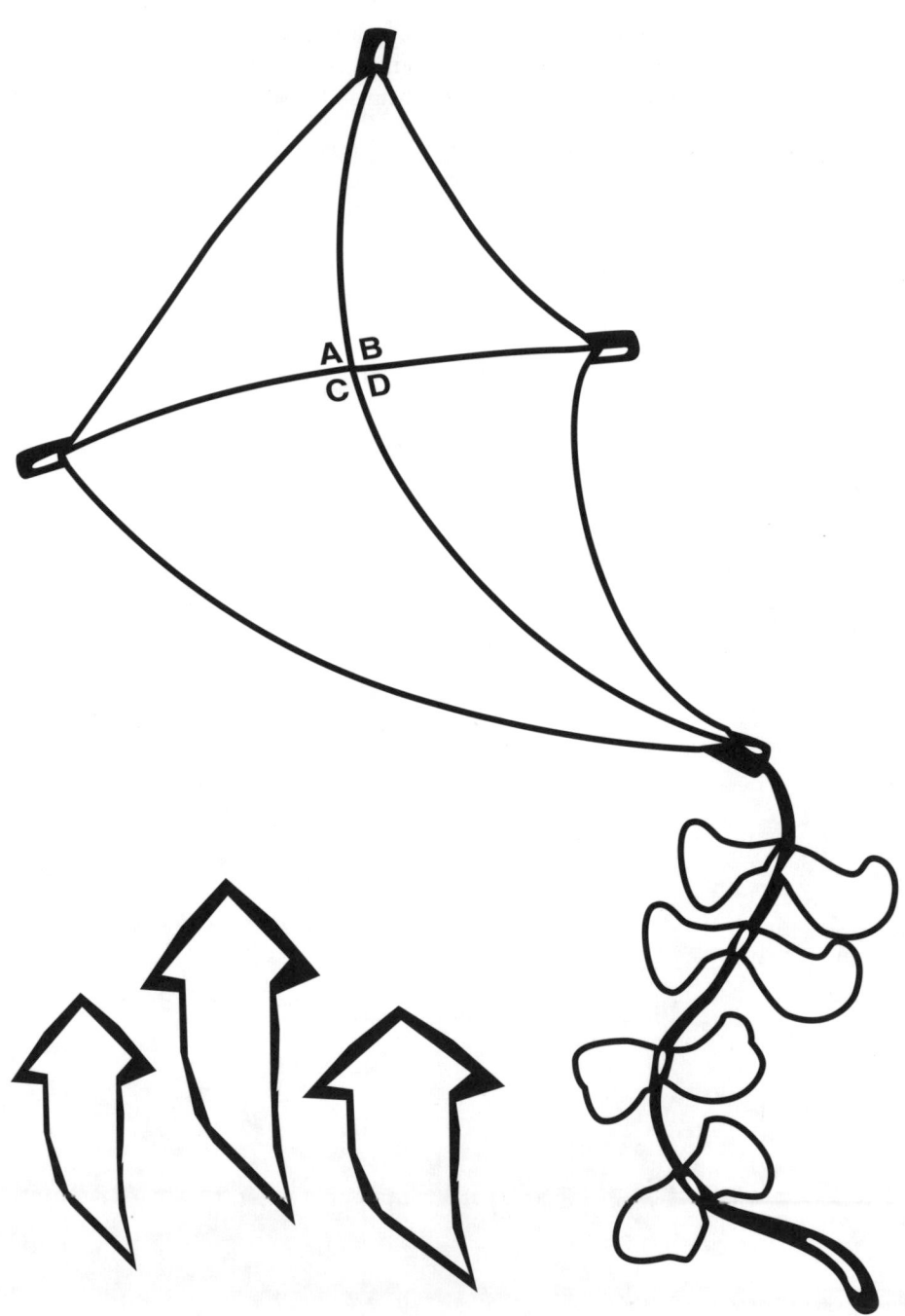

©1995 Whole Person Press 210 W Michigan Duluth MN 55802   (800) 247-6789

168 HOPE CHEST

Participants fill their chests with all their hopes for change in this thoughtful, upbeat exercise.

GOALS

To identify goals for change.

To plan for ways to accomplish these goals.

GROUP SIZE

Unlimited.

TIME FRAME

15–20 minutes

MATERIALS NEEDED

Hope Chest worksheet.

PROCESS

1) The trainer distributes **Hope Chest** worksheets and guides participants through a process for reflecting on their hopes for change.

   ➤ Think about what you have learned about stress in this session. How do you want to apply these insights and ideas to your own life? What changes do you hope to make?

   ➤ Write down your hopes for change in your **Hope Chest**.

   ➤ Be as specific and concrete and possible! (For example, instead of "feel good," write "find something to laugh about everyday" or "express gratitude and appreciation to others daily.")

   ➤ Write your name on the **Hope Chest**.

2) When participants have filled their hope chests, the trainer asks them to return to their small groups and then guides them through a process for sharing.

   ➤ Spotlight each person in the group one by one.

   ➤ The person in the spotlight should tell about your hopes for change, explain why you want these changes, and describe the steps you will take to make these hopes a reality.

➤ The person whose parents have been married the longest begins.

3) When participants have finished sharing their hopes for change, the trainer concludes by thanking people for their participation in group, and wishing them well in their efforts toward realizing their hopes.

VARIATIONS

■ As part of *Step 2*, group members share their hopes for each other and add them to each person's **Hope Chest**.

TRAINER'S NOTES

HOPE CHEST

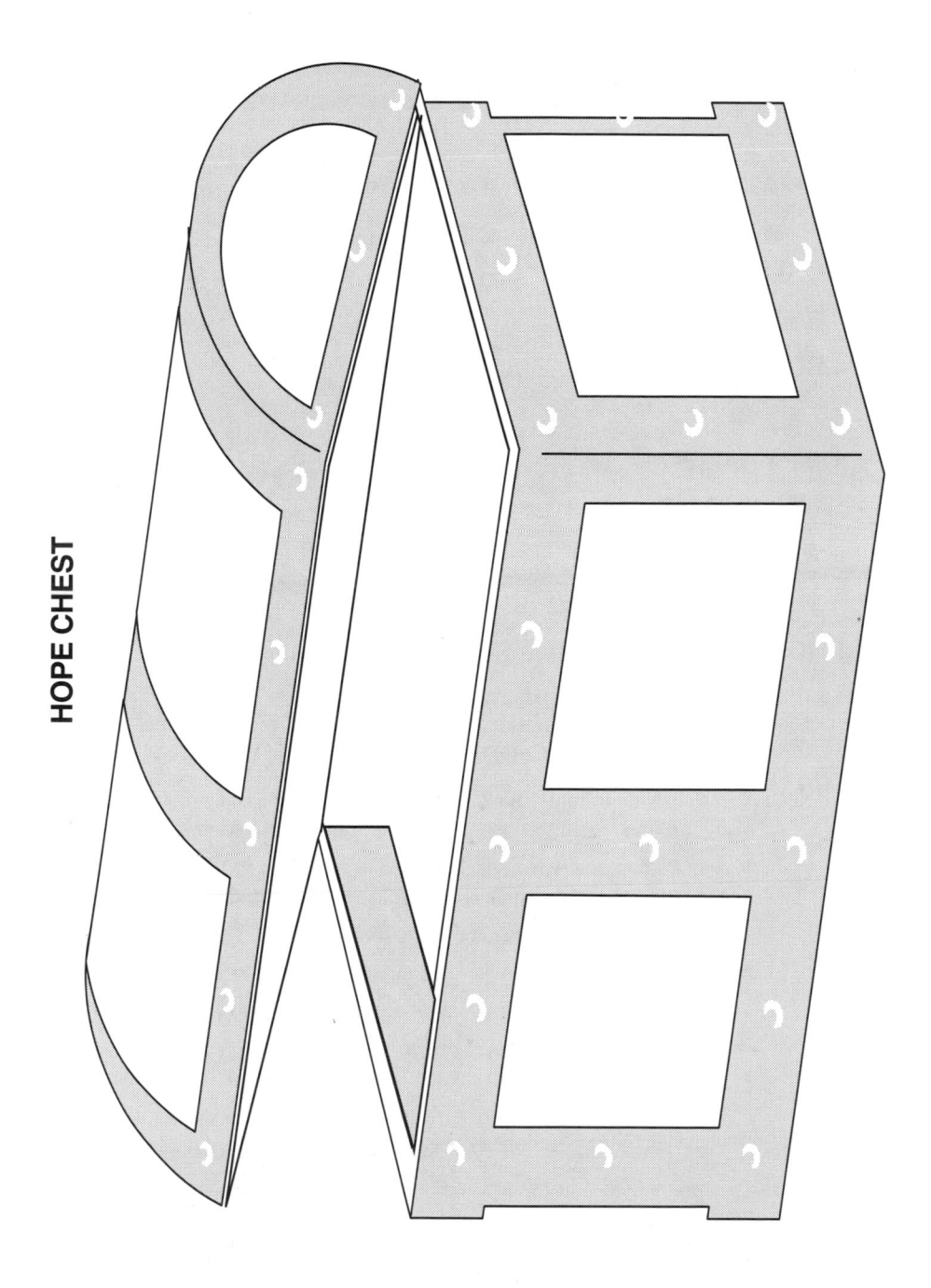

169 KEY LEARNING

In this simple, effective process for closure and planning, participants write important insights and personal applications on three keys which will open the door for change.

GOALS

To summarize learning and apply ideas to current life situations.

GROUP SIZE

Unlimited.

TIME FRAME

5–10 minutes

MATERIALS NEEDED

Key Learning worksheets; newsprint easel and markers.

PROCESS

1) The trainer invites participants to brainstorm a list of key content ideas from their learning experience, writing all insights on newsprint as group members describe the highlights.

2) The trainer distributes **Key Learning** worksheets and guides participants through the three-step process for closure and planning.

   ➤ Think about the learnings generated in this group, and focus on what has been most important or helpful to you at this time in your life.

   ➤ Write your key learning in the top key.

   ➤ Now think about how you can apply this learning to your current life.

   ➤ Write your ideas about applying what you have learned in the second key.

   ➤ Now think about what else you need to do to bring about the changes you described in the middle key.

   ➤ Write your plans for action in the bottom key.

3) The trainer asks participants to rejoin their small groups and share their key responses.

   ➤ Each person describe your keys in a quick go-around the group.

©1995 Whole Person Press 210 W Michigan Duluth MN 55802   (800) 247-6789

4) When all have had the opportunity to talk about their key learnings, the trainer concludes by encouraging participants to use their keys to open doors for healthy change.

VARIATIONS

■ In longer learning experiences or workshops, participants could fill out a key learning sheet for each new session and accumulate them throughout the day. Then at the end, all of these keys could be stapled together in a book of learning to take home.

TRAINER'S NOTES

KEY LEARNING

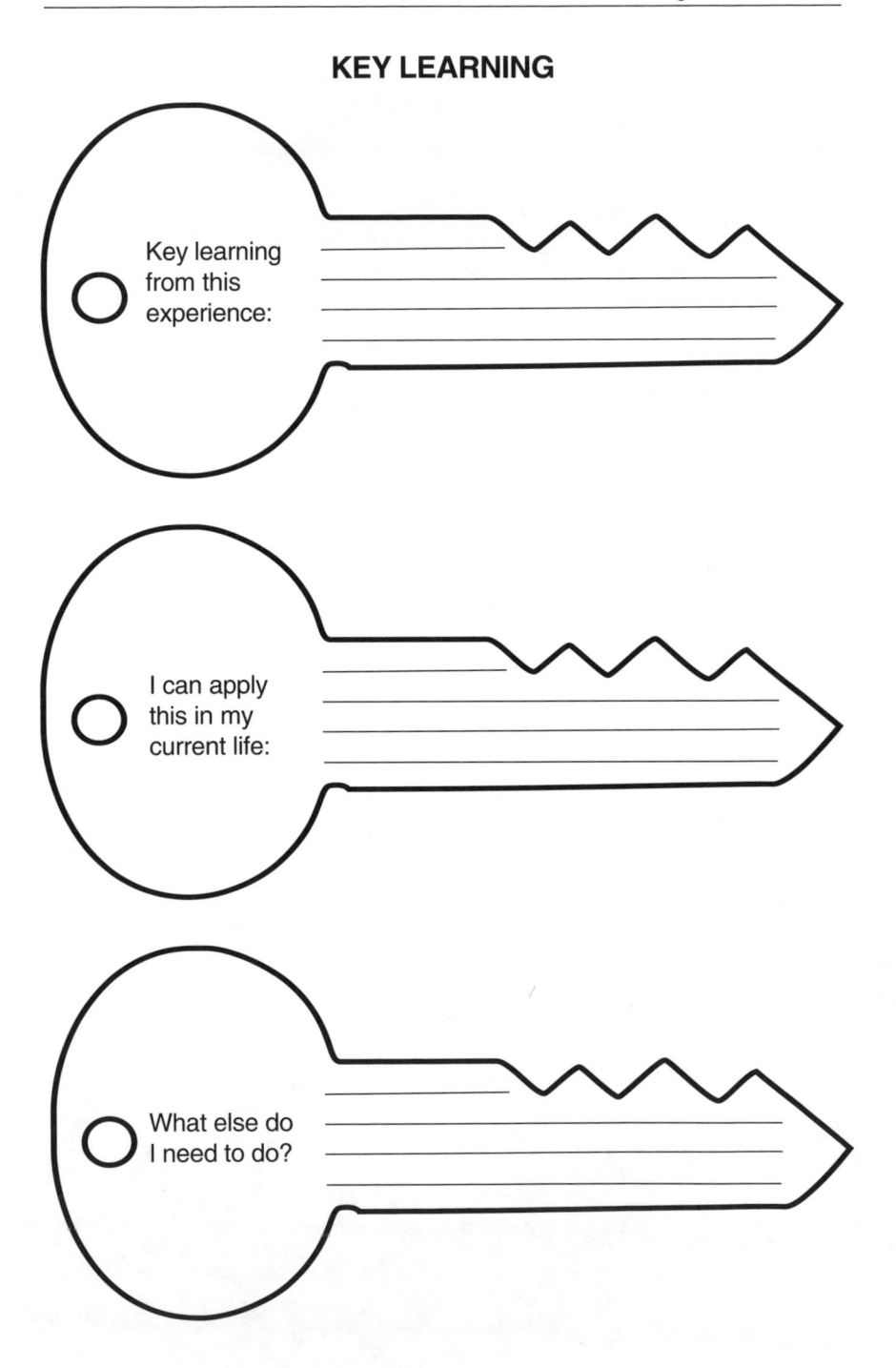

Key learning
from this
experience:

I can apply
this in my
current life:

What else do
I need to do?

170 STRESS EXAMINER

In this creative, playful exercise, participants imagine the contents of a stress management newspaper that provides exactly the kind of information they need for healthy living.

GOALS

To summarize learnings about stress management.

To identify resources needed for personal change.

GROUP SIZE

Unlimited.

TIME FRAME

20–30 minutes.

MATERIALS NEEDED

Large, blank sheets of paper and colored markers for each participant.

PROCESS

1) The trainer invites participants to consider this scenario.

   ➤ Imagine that a self-help newspaper called the *Stress Examiner* has just been delivered to your door.

      ➤ This newspaper includes exactly the information you need for stress management at this time in your life.

      ➤ It incorporates the learning you have gained today, plus tips for how to apply this information as you plan for change in the future.

   ➤ Think about the contents of this newspaper.

      ➤ What will be the headline?

      ➤ What sections, articles, columns, advertisements, cartoons, and other material will you include?

      ➤ What have you learned in this course?

      ➤ What do you need to read?

2) The trainer passes out blank sheets of paper and colored makers to each participant. He then explains the next step for creating a personal *Stress Examiner*.

©1995 Whole Person Press 210 W Michigan Duluth MN 55802   (900) 017 0700

➤ Use this paper to design the front page of your newspaper.

➤ Write your own headline for the paper.

➢ This may be an important concept for stress management, a new insight, or any other valuable news that you want to highlight.

➤ Decide on one or two other articles you consider worthy of front page space. Write their titles and a brief description of their contents.

➤ Write a table of contents for your paper, briefly describing the main sections, columns, and articles included.

➤ Add any cartoons or advertising that you want to include in your paper.

➢ Be creative and have fun.

➤ You will have 10 minutes to develop your paper.

➢ If you have extra time, add more pages or sections to your paper, designing more fully what you outlined in the table of contents.

3) After about 10 minutes the trainer interrupts and asks participants to rejoin their small groups from earlier in the session. When everyone is settled, he invites them to focus on a personal goal for change.

➤ Find a spot on your newspaper to write one of your goals for change.

➢ Use the format: *In six months, the headline of my newspaper will be . . .*

➤ Each person in turn show your newspaper to the group.

➢ Describe the contents of your paper and explain why you included each item.

➢ Then read the headline for six months from now.

4) As a closing summary, the trainer reconvenes the group and invites participants to share headlines and topics covered in their newspapers with the large group.

VARIATIONS

■ Add a "Letters to the Editor" section in each paper. Where individuals receive personal written letters of affirmation from everyone in the small group.

Group
Energizers

171 ANTI-STRESS COFFEE BREAK

Participants fill their tanks with energizing foods and beverages, instead of stress foods like caffeine and sugars.

GOALS

To provide participants with foods which nourish their bodies and restore feelings of vitality.

GROUP SIZE

Unlimited.

TIME FRAME

10–15 minutes

MATERIALS NEEDED

Anti-stress foods prepared in advance for all participants: raw fruits (bananas, apples, oranges), raw vegetables (broccoli, carrots, celery, cauliflower), whole grain bread, muffins, or bagels, raisins, lowfat yogurt, wild rice salad, pasta salad, blanched almonds, skim milk, herbal teas, fresh lemon slices, and water (hot and cold).

Coffee Anthem lyrics on poster, overhead or handouts.

PROCESS

☞ *This experience is most appropriate for an afternoon break in a longer workshop and would be a nice match for workshops on stress, nutrition and self care.*

1) The trainer announces that it is time for a break so that participants can refuel their bodies and restore their energy. The trainer explains that since this will be an **anti-stress coffee break**, foods and beverages that stress their bodies and minds were eliminated.

   ● The anti-stress coffee break does not include coffee. Caffeine is a stimulant which pumps adrenaline into your body and stresses your heart, liver, and kidneys. While it may make us feel pumped up, it actually drains energy, leaving us feeling fatigued, less able to concentrate, irritable, and nervous.

2) The trainer points out that in spite of its negative effects, coffee is a social lubricant popular around the world. He challenges participants to join him in a song lamenting the loss of this old friend, caffeine. He passes our copies of the Coffee Anthem and leads group members through the song.

➤ Stand up and place your hand over your heart.

➤ Sing the song to the tune of the Star Spangled Banner.

➤ Sing loudly, with gusto.

3) When the song is over, the trainer invites participants to experiment with some alternative social lubricants among the stress-free snacks provided.

The Coffee Anthem *was written by David and Anne Frähm, authors of* **Healthy Habits: 20 Simple Ways to Improve Your Health** *(Colorado Springs: Pinon Press, 1993).*

COFFEE ANTHEM Script

Oh say can you see,
my cup of coffee?

It's the stuff that I need
for my fix of caffeine!

Without it I'm a mess,
my head is distressed.

My mind is all shot
'til I've had half a pot.

Oh, but now I've found it,
my headache has quit.
My brain has kicked in,
I am human again.

Oh, please don't ever try to take
caffeine away from me.

It's the drug that we crave most,
in the land of the free.

172 BREATH PRAYER

Participants tap into their inner healing resources in this relaxing, rhythmic, affirmation meditation.

GOALS

To provide relaxation and centering.

To identify and affirm core truths.

GROUP SIZE

Unlimited.

TIME FRAME

8–10 minutes

MATERIALS NEEDED

Breath Prayer script.

PROCESS

1) The trainer gives some background to the spiritual dimension of breathing.

   ● In many languages the word for "spirit" and "breath" are the same. In Hebrew, the word is *ruach*. In Greek, *pneuma*. The root word for "inspiration" is *inspire*, to breathe in.

   ● Most religious traditions include breathing/meditation routines for individual or group spiritual experience, ranging from Gregorian chant to Yoga, to St. Ambrose's thought prayers, to Hindu mantras, to Native American chants, to the Jesus prayer immortalized in JD Salinger's *Franny and Zooey*.

   ● Breathing opens us to the spiritual dimension of our being.

2) The trainer introduces the concept of the **breath prayer** affirmation.

   ● A **breath prayer** is a repeated mental review of a meaningful phrase. The phrase could be a brief affirmation of oneself, a statement of an eternal truth, a petition, an image of a desired attitude, a proclamation of personal commitment, an aspiration or goal.

©1995 Whole Person Press 210 W Michigan Duluth MN 55802   (800) 247-6789

● The breath prayer phrase should easily divide in half for inhalation and exhalation, so you can mentally say the affirmation in rhythm with your breathing.

3) The trainer invites participants to brainstorm individually possible breath prayer affirmations that would be meaningful to them.

☞ *Give examples to prime the pump as needed:*

I am . . . At peace	*Fill me . . . Use me*
I am filled . . . With love	*Be still . . . Know God*
I am . . . Alive	*Heal . . . Me*
I forgive . . . Myself	*God . . . Loves me*
I am . . . Healing	*Let go . . . Let God*
I am . . . Renewed	*I am . . . Joyous*

4) The trainer asks for examples of breath prayer phrases and encourages participants to jot down appealing ideas suggested by others.

5) Participants are invited to choose a personal affirmation to use in their **breath prayer**.

6) The trainer reads the **Breath Prayer** script.

7) The trainer solicits reactions to the meditation and encourages participants to experiment with using this technique in stressful situations or as a daily attunement exercise, changing the affirmation phrase as needed.

BREATH PRAYER Script

Settle back comfortably now and begin to tune in to your body . . .
Stretch any part of your body that feels tight or tense . . .
Stretching and releasing . . .
Allowing any tension or tightness to free itself
with the gentle movements of your stretch . . .

Close your eyes now . . .
Begin to tune out the noise and distractions of your environment . . .
Prepare to tune in to your inner silence . . .

Allow your focus to shift now to your breathing . . .
Pay attention to the easy, steady flow of your breath . . .
in and out . . . in and out . . .
as you breathe slowly and deeply . . .
listening to the quiet of your life-giving breath . . .

☞ *Pause 10 seconds.*

As you continue to breathe with slow, full breaths . . .
begin to focus on the phrase I AM CALM . . .
hearing in your mind I AM as you inhale . . .
and as you exhale . . . mentally hearing CALM . . .
I AM as you inhale . . .
CALM as you exhale . . .
Continue to hear this affirmation as you inhale and exhale ten times . . .

☞ *Pause 45–50 seconds, gauging by your own ten deep*
breaths.

And now allow your own breath prayer to come into your mind . . .
It may be the phrase you chose earlier . . .
or a new affirming prayer may come to you . . .
or you may continue with the I AM . . . CALM . . .

On your next inhalation . . . allow your healing phrase to come to mind . . .
and continue for ten breaths or more . . .
praying in rhythm with your own breathing . . .

☞ *Pause one minute.*

Now let your mental voice grow softer and softer . . .
as your attention shifts once again to the present time and this place . . .
bringing back with you the relaxation . . . peace . . . and healing . . .
you have experienced . . .

As you inhale . . . stretch your hands and your feet . . .
Begin to become aware of the environment around you . . .
Tune in to the sounds . . .
Become aware of the other people nearby . . .
Yet stay in touch with your profound sense of peace and centeredness . . .

☞ *Pause 10 seconds.*

When you are ready . . . open your eyes . . . and rejoin the group . . .
bringing with you the spirit of truth you have rediscovered . . .

173 COBRA

This gentle Yoga movement stretches the back muscles, expands the chest and stimulates the inner organs.

GOALS

To reduce tension and release trapped energy.

To promote flexibility and resiliency.

GROUP SIZE

Unlimited as long as there in appropriate space for everyone to stretch out comfortably on the floor.

TIME FRAME

5 minutes

MATERIALS NEEDED

Cobra script; individual exercise mats or at least a clean carpet.

PROCESS

☞ *This stretch in not appropriate for formal settings or after a meal. Loose, informal clothing and an empty stomach are best.*

1) The trainer invites participants to spread around the room and find a comfortable place to lie down for the cobra pose.

   ☞ *If more introduction is needed, use the introductory chalktalk from* **Yoga** *(p 94).*

   Remind participants that this should be a gentle stretch in slow motion, not calisthenics or a race.

2) The trainer guides the group through the **Cobra Stretch** script.

©1995 Whole Person Press 210 W Michigan Duluth MN 55802   (800) 247-6789

COBRA Script

This yoga posture is called Bhujangasana or the cobra.

Begin by lying down on your stomach . . .
with your forehead resting on the mat . . . arms at your sides . . .
Allow your body to ease into the pose . . .
Allow your body to relax as much as possible . . .
let the tension flow out of your muscles as you relax.
**

Now bring your hands up and place them between your shoulders . . .
with palms flat on the floor and fingertips touching under your chin . . .
Keep your elbows comfortably close to your rib cage . . .
Now bring your legs and ankles together and point your toes.

To begin your stretch, imagine that you are in a super slow motion video.
Very slowly raise your head . . .
feeling each vertebra slowly move as you allow your neck to arch . . .
Ease into this stretch . . . don't push . . .
Hold it for five seconds.

Now, continuing in super slow motion, begin to raise your chest . . .
pushing against the floor with your hands for support . . .
Again, ease into this stretch very slowly and don't push . . .
Allow yourself to relax for five seconds.

Now, staying in super slow motion . . .
continue to raise your trunk off the floor . . .
allowing your spine to arch gracefully and easily . . . vertebra by vertebra . . .
Your head should be arched back . . . your eyes looking upward . . .
elbows slightly bent . . . spine arched . . . legs relaxed . . .
Hold this pose for a count of ten.

Now once again in super slow motion . . .
reverse your movement and lower your trunk . . . chest . . . and head . . .
until you are back to the original position . . .
relaxing deeply with your forehead on the floor . . .
and your arms alongside your body . . .
letting your body go completely limp.

Close your eyes and rest for a moment.

And now repeat the sequence.

> ☞ *Begin the script again at the **. Remind people to move*
> *slowly, without jerking, relying on back muscles to lift*
> *and arm muscles to support.*

174 HAND DANCING

Even those what hate to dance will love this playful, easy process for mimicking a partner's hand movements to music.

GOALS

To get energized.

To feel connected to other group members.

GROUP SIZE

Works best with groups larger than 8 people.

TIME FRAME

10 minutes

MATERIALS NEEDED

Lively music to play during the dancing exercise.

PROCESS

1) The trainer introduces the exercise by asking participants to indicate by a show of hands how many people enjoy dancing. He affirms those who responded positively, and then reassures those who did not raise their hands that this is a dance that they might enjoy, since they can perform it without moving their feet.

2) The trainer asks participants to stand up and find a partner (or trio, if their are odd numbers of group members) who is wearing shoes similar to their own.

   ☞ *If some people can't find a match, tell them to pair up with someone else who has uncommon shoes.*

3) When everyone has a partner, the trainer explains how the dance works.

   ➤ Face your partner, standing about two feet apart.

   ➤ Decide who will be *Fred Astaire* and who will be *Ginger Rogers*.

   ☞ *Groups with three people will have two Gingers or two Freds.*

   ➤ *Fred Astaire* will take the lead role for the first dance.

   ➤ *Ginger Rogers* will follow the moves of Fred Astaire.

> ➤ When the music starts, **Fred Astaires** should use your hands to create a dance, which the Ginger Rogers will follow.
>
>> ➤ **Gingers**, imitate Fred's movements exactly as if you were a mirror image.
>
> ➤ Be as creative and lively as you can, using your hands to express your feelings.

4) When participants understand the instructions, the trainer starts the music and tells them to start their dance.

5) After about two minutes, the trainer signals that it's time to switch roles so **Ginger Rogers** become the leaders of the dance and **Fred Astaires** are the followers.

6) When the second dance is finished, the trainer asks dancing partners to discuss two questions. (2 minutes)

> ➤ What was it like to be the leader, and have someone watching and following your every move?
>
> ➤ What was it like to the follower, and to allow another person to control your movements?

7) In conclusion, the trainer invites general comments from the group about their comfort level with the roles of leader and follower, summarizes their responses, and compliments people on their willingness to try out both roles.

VARIATIONS

■ This exercise would be ideal for groups focused on leadership, or for women's groups discussing roles and assertiveness.

■ Incorporate this routine into *Lifetrap 5: Superwoman*, p 22.

175 HUMMING BREATH

Participants enjoy a relaxing internal massage as they practice a mystical, musical Yoga technique for reducing tension.

GOALS

To relax and get centered.

To experiment with an alternative technique for coping with stress.

GROUP SIZE

Unlimited.

TIME FRAME

3–5 minutes

PROCESS

1) The trainer provides a brief introduction to the value of humming as a stress reliever.

   ● One of the simplest body/mind/spirit techniques for stress relief is one of the most ancient ones as well, dating back to ancient Yoga practices—humming.

   ● Focusing on the humming breath clears the mind, slows down and deepens breathing, and leads to a relaxing, meditative state.

   ● Humming helps us tap into the healing power of music, while at the same time providing a delightful internal massage for the breathing passageways, relaxing these muscles through vibration.

   ● Humming as a group reinforces out sense of connectedness to our neighbors and oneness with all creation.

2) The trainer invites participants to demonstrate their humming ability by humming a tune together.

   ☞ *Identify the person whose birthday is closest to today and hum* **Happy Birthday**. *Or choose another familiar tune that fits your audience or the time of year. Encourage people to hum loudly, not to worry about being on tune.*

3) Now that everyone is warmed up to humming, the trainer directs participants to try a spontaneous one-note hum.

➤ On the count of three, each person should start humming your own personal hum.

➤ The pitch and the volume don't matter, just find your own note and hum it.

☞ *Count to three and hum. Encourage people to extend the hum for 15–30 seconds, taking a breath as needed.*

4) The trainer leads the group through the Yoga breath and humming sequence.

➤ Close your eyes and relax as much as possible.

➤ Take several deep breaths.

➤ Breathe in easily through your nose.

➤ As you breathe out, extend your breath fully, emptying your lungs completely.

➤ With each succeeding breath, extend your exhale a little further and longer.

☞ *Allow time for at least three deep breaths.*

➤ On the next breath, close your lips and make a long, **high** humming sound as you exhale.

☞ *Help the group get started by humming yourself. Each hum can be repeated three times, or you can do one breath for each hum and then repeat the sequence.*

➤ On the next breath, exhale with a long **low** humming sound..

➤ On the next breath, exhale with a **very loud** humming sound.

➤ On the next breath, exhale with a **soft and sweet** humming sound.

➤ On the next breath, exhale **without any sound**, and listen to the silence.

5) Participants are invited to share observations and insights with the group.

Inspiration for this technique came from Kenneth K Cohen's delightful Yoga picture book for children, **Imagine That!** *(Santa Barbara CA: Santa Barbara Books, 1983)*

176 STRESS SQUEEZERS

In this humorous activity participants reflect on their stress levels and coping styles as they sculpt a personalized desktop stress reducer.

GOALS

To identify life stressors.

To explore symbolic and physical tension relief.

GROUP SIZE

The more the merrier, as long as there is space for group filling stations.

TIME FRAME

10–15 minutes

MATERIALS NEEDED

For each participant: one large, sturdy, light-colored balloon (available at toy or party goods store) and a fine point permanent magic marker (various colors). For each group filling station: one plastic funnel, bucket or bag of playbox sand (a 50-pound bag of sand costs less than $5.00 and will make about 150 squeezers).

PROCESS

☞ *In advance of this activity, prepare a sand bucket "filling station" for each team of 3–6 participants.*

1) The trainer divides the group into teams of 3 to 6 participants and instructs teams to gather at their respective filling stations around the room.

   ☞ *Be creative in dividing into teams (eg, by make or year of family car) and naming the filling stations (eg, after oil companies).*

2) The trainer gives instructions for making personal stress squeezers.

   ➤ Each person should take a balloon and magic marker.

   ➤ Think about some of the stressful aspects, situations, or people in your daily life.

   ➤ Using the marker and words, abbreviations, or symbols, cover your balloon with the stresses of your daily life. Be sure not to puncture the balloon.

➤ You may want to use different colors for home stress, work stress, community stress, or physical stress. Just exchange markers with others on your team.

➤ Feel free to talk with others as you identify your stress.

☞ *Allow 3–5 minutes for this step. Encourage people along the way, reminding them of possible stress sources, listening in, and reporting to other teams. Interrupt when most people have finished decorating.*

➤ Now, cooperate as a group to fill your balloons with sand, using the funnel provided.

➤ Fill the balloon with sand until it fits comfortably in the palm of your hand—about the size of a lemon.

➤ Squeeze out any air and tie the top

3) The trainer invites participants to try their stress squeezers.

➤ Take turns talking about your stress with others on your team.

➤ As you describe some of the stresses of your life, experiment with poking and prodding your sculpture.

➤ Take 5 minutes to play and compare notes about your stresses.

4) The trainer reconvenes the large group and solicits insights, applications, and reactions, using these to frame a closing challenge or transition to the next content segment.

● Play with your stress squeezer for two minutes anytime you feel stressed on the job this week. Talk to it, shape it, do what comes naturally.

● Pay attention to your feelings as you squeeze, focusing on discharging or releasing the stress.

● Stress Squeezers are not indestructible! Don't use yours near a keyboard.

VARIATIONS

■ As part of a health fair or EAP wellness promotion day, invite participants or employees to stop by and make their own executive toys for stress management.

■ Make stress squeezers to advertise upcoming stress management courses or programs—just have the dates and times printed on the balloons before filling with sand.

Submitted by Julie Lusk.

177 SUPERMAN

In this tongue-in-cheek discussion of performance and perfectionism, men and women are challenged to accept their imperfection and learn from their mistakes.

GOALS

To recognize that everyone makes mistakes.

To learn from our mistakes.

GROUP SIZES

Unlimited.

TIME FRAME

5–10 minutes

MATERIALS NEEDED

One blank sheet of paper and writing utensils for each participant; copies of the **Performance Rating Guide** for all.

PROCESS

☞ *This energizer is a perfect companion to* **Lifetrap 5: Superwoman,** *p 22.*

1) The trainer provides a warm-up to this exercise by asking participants if anyone in the group made a small mistake today. He invites volunteers to share examples of minor mistakes made in their day, and goes on to ask if anyone in the group has ever made a mistake, making the point that mistakes are unavoidable because we are human.

2) The trainer distributes blank paper and informs the group that everyone will have the opportunity to practice making mistakes—and have fun doing it.

   ➤ Pair up with a neighbor to share this humbling experience.

   ➤ In 30 seconds, draw a detailed picture of anything you want, using your opposite (non-writing) hand.

   ➤ When you are finished, show your picture to your partner and ask her to guess what your drawing is supposed to be.

☞ *This will inevitably cause laughter as people see their wild drawings.*

3) The trainer gives instructions for a second drawing.

➤ This time you can use your usual writing hand.

➤ Take 30 seconds to draw a picture of your partner's face, keeping your eyes closed as you draw.

➤ When you are finished, show your drawing to your partner.

4) The trainer passes out copies of the **Performance Rating Guide**, and suggests that participants look it over and decide how they would rate their performance in this exercise.

5) The trainer concludes by encouraging participants to continue to seek excellence, and live with and laugh at their imperfections.

● It is very stressful to avoid, deny, divert responsibility for human errors. It is better to face mistakes, accept them, correct them, learn from them, and move on from the experience.

VARIATIONS

■ This exercise is an effective companion to *Lifetrap 5: Superwoman*, p 22.

TRAINER'S NOTES

Submitted by Joel Goodman.

©1995 Whole Person Press £ IU W Michigan Duluth MN 55802   (800) 247-6789

©1995 Whole Person Press 210 W Michigan Duluth MN 55802 (800) 247-6789

PERFORMANCE RATING GUIDE

PERFORMANCE Far exceeds job requirements	Exceeds job requirements	Meets job requirements	Needs some improvement	Does not meet minimum requirements
QUALITY Leaps tall buildings with a single bound	Must take running start to leap over tall buildings	Can leap over short buildings only	Crashes into buildings when attempting to jump over them	Cannot recognize buildings at all
TIMELINESS Is faster than a speeding bullet	Is as fast as a speeding bullet	Not quite as fast as a speeding bullet	Would you believe a slow bullet	Wounds self with bullet when attempting to shoot
INITIATIVE Is stronger than a locomotive	Is stronger than an elephant	Is stronger than a bull	Shoots the bull	Smells like a bull
ADAPTABILITY Walks on water consistently	Walks on water in emergencies	Washes with water	Drinks water	Passes water in emergencies
COMMUNICATIONS Talks with God	Talks with the angels	Talks to himself	Argues with himself	Loses these arguments

SUPERMAN

178 TOO BAD!

Participants poke gentle fun at themselves and each other by taking turns complaining and sympathizing about life's minor hassles.

GOALS

To recognize that everyone has frustrations in life.

To learn not to take problems too seriously.

To shift from a complaining mode to a coping mode.

GROUP SIZE

Unlimited.

TIME FRAME

10–15 minutes

PROCESS

1) The trainer invites participants to let off steam about one of their stresses.

   ➤ Pair up with someone you don't know.

      ➤ Decide who will be **Moan** and who will be **Groan**.

      ➤ **Moans** will begin.

   ➤ **Moans**, tell your partner about a recent hassle in your life that has caused you stress and frustration.

      ➤ You could choose a type of stress: relationships, work pressures, family demands, obligations, etc.

      ➤ Pick a hassle that is a common, daily stressor, not a major life stress.

         ☞ *Point out that life is tough. We all have lots of frustrations and deserve sympathy.*

   ➤ **Groans**, your job is to sympathize with your partner by saying, "Oh, too bad . . ." in response to each complaint.

   ➤ **Moans**, this is your chance to complain to a sympathetic audience. You have one minute, go ahead and gripe.

      ☞ *Interrupt after a minute and instruct partners to switch roles.*

   ➤ This time **Groans** complain and **Moans** sympathize.

2) The trainer asks for examples of gripes from several pairs and uses these as a bridge to the next step.

- Although it's nice to have a sympathetic ear for our griping, we need to remember that EVERYONE has problems. People often become so absorbed in life situations they begin to think they're the only one facing tough situations.

- In fact, there is not a person in the room who is not dealing with something they don't like, but that's the way life is!! And all the griping in the world won't change it.

3) The trainer instructs pairs to try the complaining exercise again.

➤ *Moans*, choose another minor hassle to grip about.

➤ *Groans*, this time take a more callous attitude, changing to a less sympathetic tone of voice as you respond "Too bad!"—so you communicate "Tough cookies! Everyone has problems."

☞ *Give the signal to start and keep time for one minute. Then switch partners and repeat.*

4) After the group has had a chance to try out unsympathetic responses, the trainer challenges participants to think about their reactions to both responses, and the kind of response they would have preferred.

➤ Discuss your reactions to both responses, and then describe the kind of response you wanted from your partner.

➤ Each person has two minutes to share.

5) The trainer solicits insights from participants to share with the large group, summarizes these ideas, and points out how humor and knowing you are not alone helps people put their problems in perspective.

Submitted by Pat Miller.

©1995 Whole Person Press 210 W Michigan Duluth MN 55802   (800) 247-6789

179 TROUBLE BUBBLES

This short visualization allows participants to get rid of negative feelings by imagining them as bubbles that they blow away.

GOALS

To let go of stressful thoughts and feelings.

GROUP SIZE

Unlimited; also appropriate for individuals.

TIME FRAME

5–10 minutes

MATERIALS NEEDED

Trouble Bubbles script and relaxing music to use as background.

PROCESS

1) The trainer informs participants that they will have the opportunity to let go of stress by imagining their troubles as bubbles they can blow away.

2) The trainer suggests that everyone finds a place and position in the room where they feel comfortable.

   ☞ *Ideally, participants could lie down on a clean, carpeted floor. If this is not possible, encourage them to relax in their chairs, remove glasses, and set their papers on the floor.*

3) When everyone is comfortable, the trainer dims the lights, plays soft music, and reads the **Trouble Bubbles** script.

4) When the script has ended, the trainer allows participants time to walk around, stretch, and slowly return their attention to the next agenda.

Submitted by Mel Wittmer.

©1995 Whole Person Press 210 W Michigan Duluth MN 55802   (800) 247-6789

TROUBLE BUBBLES Script

Find a place where your body feels comfortable and supported . . .
Close your eyes . . .
and allow your whole body to relax . . .
Breathe in and out slowly . . .
deeply . . . evenly . . .

Become aware of any bad feelings you have . . .
as you review what has happened to you today . . .
They may be feelings of sadness . . .
loneliness . . . anxiousness . . . anger . . . or guilt . . .
Tune into whatever undesirable feelings you recall . . .

☞ *Pause 5 seconds*

Now let these bad feelings . . .
and the thoughts that go with them . . .
become bubbles in your mind . . .

☞ *Pause 15 seconds*

Imagine as you exhale . . .
that you blow these bubbles of bad feelings away . . .
Try exhaling with your mouth open . . .
so you hear the sound of the air rushing out . . .
as you blow away the bubbles . . .

☞ *Pause 15 seconds*

Continue to breathe and blow . . .
until you can no longer see the bubbles or feel the feelings . . .
Some have broken . . .
others have drifted out of sight . . .
You feel free and light . . .
very much alive . . .

☞ *Pause 15 seconds*

Now, when you are ready, slowly return to your surroundings . . .
carrying this feeling of lightness and energy back with you . . .

☞ *Pause 5 seconds*

When you open your eyes you will feel refreshed and free.

180 TRY, TRY AGAIN

This surprising parable underlines the importance of developing a wide repertoire of coping strategies for managing stress.

GOALS

To reinforce new problem solving skills.

To poke fun at people's propensity for intensity.

TIME FRAME

5 minutes

MATERIALS NEEDED

Try, Try Again script.

PROCESS

1) The trainer introduces the reading, making appropriate bridges to previous or upcoming content, if desired.

2) The trainer reads the **Try, Try Again** script.

3) After the reading, the trainer solicits reaction from the group, and asks for "testimonials" from people who have felt like the fly batting against the window pane. As participants respond, the trainer reinforces the connection between this parable and stress management.

- **Most of us are lazy stress managers.** We tend to rely on one or two familiar strategies for tackling life issues. And once committed to a particular strategy, we usually keep trying it over and over, even when it's not working.

- In most stressful situations, we would be well advised to look for the open door which is probably close by, if only we will try a new direction.

- The more skills we have in our coping repertoire, the more likely we are to try another approach rather than trying harder.

Submitted by Price Pritchett.

©1995 Whole Person Press 210 W Michigan Duluth MN 55802   (800) 247-6789

TRY, TRY AGAIN Script

I'm sitting in a quiet room at the Milcroft Inn, a peaceful little place hidden back among the pine trees about an hour out of Toronto. It's just past noon, late July, and I'm listening to the desperate sounds of a life-or-death struggle going on a few feet away.

There's a small fly burning out the last of its short life's energies in a futile attempt to fly through the glass of the windowpane. The whining wings tell the poignant story of the fly's strategy: Try harder.

But it's not working.

The frenzied effort offers no hope for survival. Ironically, the struggle is part of the trap. It is impossible for the fly to try hard enough to succeed at breaking through the glass. Nevertheless, this little insect has staked its life on reaching its goal through raw effort and determination.

This fly is doomed. It will die there on the windowsill.

Across the room, ten steps away, the door is open. Ten seconds of flying time and this small creature could reach the outside world it seeks. With only a fraction of the effort now being wasted, it could be free of this self-imposed trap. The breakthrough possibility is there. It would be so easy.

Why doesn't the fly try another approach, something dramatically different? How did it get so locked in on the idea that this particular route and determined effort offer the most promise for success? What logic is there in continuing until death to seek a breakthrough with more of the same?

No doubt this approach makes sense to the fly. Regrettably, it's an idea that will kill.

Trying harder isn't necessarily the solution to achieving more. It may not offer any real promise for getting what you want out of life. Sometimes, in fact, it's a big part of the problem.

If you stake your hopes for a breakthrough on trying harder than ever, you may kill your chances for success.

By Price Pritchett from **Chicken Soup for the Soul** *(Winter Park FL: Health Communications Inc, 1993).*

©1995 Whole Person Press 210 W Michigan Duluth MN 55802   (800) 247-6789

Resources

GUIDE TO THE RESOURCES SECTION

This resources section is intended to provide assistance for planning and preparation as you develop and expand your stress management training and consulting in various settings.

TIPS FOR TRAINERS P. 136

Ten Commandments for Ethical Training offers refresher guidelines for group leaders at all levels.

EDITORS' CHOICE p. 139

Recommendations from the editors on their favorite (FOUR****STAR) exercises from **Stress 5** and teaching designs from this volume that tackle the issue of job-related stress.

> Four****Star Exercises: The Best of **Stress 5** p. 139
> Especially for the Workplace p. 141

WINNING COMBINATIONS p. 142

Potential workshop designs using exercises from this volume. Plus notes on natural companion processes from other **Structured Exercises** volumes.

> Coping with Stress: Managing Anger and Anxiety (1–2 hours)
> Hardiness Factor Workshop (2–3 hours)
> Superwoman Stress Workshop (2–4 hours)

ANNOTATED INDEXES to Stress 5 p. 144

Guides to specific content segments and group activities incorporated in exercises from **Stress 5**, identified by page reference, time frame, brief description and comments on use.

> Index to CHALKTALKS p. 144
> Index to DEMONSTRATIONS p. 146
> Index to PHYSICAL ENERGIZERS p. 147
> Index to MENTAL ENERGIZERS p. 148
> Index to RELAXATION ROUTINES p. 149

CONTRIBUTORS/EDITORS p. 150

Data on trainers who have shared their best process ideas in this volume. All are highly skilled educators and most provide in-house training, consultation, or workshops that may be valuable to you in planning comprehensive stress management programs. Many contributors are also established authors of well-respected materials on stress, wellness, and training issues.

WHOLE PERSON PUBLICATIONS p. 153

Descriptions of trainer-tested audio, video and print resources available from the stress and wellness specialists.

TIPS FOR TRAINERS

Designing Presentations and Workshops Using Structured Exercises in Stress Management Volume 5

Whatever your professional background, from business to psychology to nursing, as a trainer you have developed an internalized set of ethical principles that guide your work. These may be so basic to you that you take them for granted, but these guidelines are vital ingredients that undergird every presentation or workshop. The **Ten Commandments for Ethical Training** may provide a consciousness-raising reminder for you.

Thou shalt do what thou said thou would do.

◆ It's tempting to offer the moon in order to close a juicy deal or to please a committee. Don't promise something you can't deliver.

◆ Show up early, know what you're doing, and do what you promised. Always have a backup plan. If an emergency makes it impossible for your to be there, provide a qualified substitute.

◆ Be clear about the training agenda, and stick to it.

Thou shalt use the power of the podium with care.

◆ Be cognizant of your influential position. Do not exploit the dependency and trust of participants. Respect their personal boundaries and need for privacy.

◆ Group dynamics can be dangerous. Encouragement and good-natured cajoling can help reluctant folks get over their anxiety, but never embarrass, manipulate, or coerce people into doing what doesn't feel good to them. For example, **Stress Management Alphabet** (Ex. 159, p. 58) includes a group backrub that should be gracefully optional.

◆ Don't toot your own horn. Affirm the contributions of participants rather than your expertise. Emphasize the learning process rather than your teaching skills. It's okay to mention your products or services briefly, but don't push them.

Thou shalt keep the group process safe for all.

◆ When planning a session, select activities that are suited to the setting and audience. Be cautious about using exercises in the workplace that may have repercussions on the individuals involved. Intense personal reflection or deep sharing probably don't belong in the workplace, except in voluntary self-help groups with trained leadership.

◆ Create a respectful, safe environment where people are accepted and not put down. Make sure the process is inclusive of all people, and that their rights are protected.

Honor all thy participants.

◆ Show respect for diverse racial, ethnic, age, status, and gender groups. Use inclusive language. Keep your examples respectful and inclusive. Maintain strict confidentiality.

◆ Be careful with humor. NEVER tell an off-color joke or use coarse language. Sexual innuendo is always offensive to someone. Please refrain. Make yourself, not participants, the target of any contextual humor.

◆ Don't let one or two people dominate the group or cause you to stray from your agenda.

◆ Listen with care to comments and questions from the audience. Always restate the contribution so everyone knows what was said—and the individual feels heard.

Thou shalt not allow bloodletting.

◆ Set limits for appropriate self-disclosure.

◆ Avoid confrontation or opening old wounds (personal or organizational) unless this is explicitly part of your contract.

◆ Finish what you start, support participants throughout the process, and provide closure.

Thou shalt refrain from involvements with participants.

◆ Maintain professional boundaries. Be friendly and personable, but limit socializing with participants before, during, and after training. Romantic or sexual intimacy with participants is a violation of their boundaries, no matter how willing they may be.

Thou shalt not steal the work of thy colleagues.

◆ Give credit where credit is due. Don't take another trainer's paradigm and present it as your own. An idea may not care who its owner is, but people who have invested their professional lives in developing ground breaking concepts, clear paradigms, clever turns of phrase, field-tested assessments, concise checklists, touching stories, provocative questions, or elegant graphic representations of complex issues deserve to be acknowledged as the originators.

◆ Be sure that every handout you distribute includes a proper citation of the source and identification of whose creative work it represents.

Thou shalt represent thyself authentically.

◆ Make up your own stories, jokes, examples, and approaches rather than "borrowing" the best of others. Develop a distinctive style of presentation that represents your own creative uniqueness.

◆ Correct any misleading or inaccurate description of your background or credentials.

Thou shalt set reasonable fees for your products and services.

◆ Give people what they are paying for—a service tailored to their specific needs and interests—rather than a canned program, or a clone of what you have developed for another group.

◆ Make your training affordable for a wide range of groups. Non-profits and small businesses need training just as badly as the Fortune 500.

Thou shalt ask permission to borrow intellectual property.

◆ Know and respect copyright laws and conventions. It is illegal to photocopy and distribute charts, checklists, concept summaries, articles, tips, cartoons, or any other material in print without specific permission from the publisher of the original work. Such permission is usually easy to obtain from the Permissions Department of the magazine, journal, or book publisher. In your written request, include information about how you plan to use the material (in a handout, publishing it in a workbook, adapting it for a worksheet, etc.) and the number of reproductions you plan to make. Some publishers have different guidelines for profit and non-profit uses. Allow 30 days for a response. Always be sure to use the proper reprint citation on every reproduction.

◆ Remember, duplicating audio or video cassettes is also illegal and unethical—no matter how easy it is! Most videotapes are intended for individual viewing only. Check with the publisher/producer for information on licensing agreements for classroom/workshop use or wide broadcast on closed-circuit or cable TV. The Whole Person video series used in Exercise 153, **Managing Job Stress** (p. 49), for example, is sold with rights for classroom (but not broadcast) use included in the price.

Thou shalt remember these commandments and keep them holy.

Give yourself a periodic ethical check-up by reviewing the **Ten Commandments** every six months. Share them with your colleagues and let these guidelines serve as a stimulus for thoughtful discussion about the complex ethical issues involved in training.

EDITORS' CHOICE

Although all 36 exercises in this volume are practical, creative, and time-tested, we must admit that we use some more than others. When people call us and ask for suggestions about which exercises to incorporate into their workshop designs we typically recommend some of our favorites—processes that have worked over and over again with many audiences, readings and activities that are guaranteed to charm a group. We call these our FOUR **** STAR choices.

Four****Star Exercise	Page	Comments (Timing)
145B Birthday Party	p. 2	Classic process with a delightful focus on birthday month stresses. Generates camaraderie and creative coping strategies for every month of the year. (5–10 min)
148 One Minute Autobiographies	p. 10	Sandy loves this adaptable technique that allows people to tell and re-tell their life story in one minute soundbites. (10–20 min)
154 Stormy Passages	p. 38	Vivid imagery of personal stress storms enables folks to put their struggles in perspective. Universal theme will touch everyone. (20–30 min)
155 Windows on Stress	p. 43	This creative problem solving technique, borrowed from our sister city in Japan, is one of Nancy's favorites. Amazing process for unfolding the layers of stress and identifying endless coping strategies. (30–45 min)
160 Yesterday, Today, Tomorrow	p. 66	The power of living in the present is a persistent theme in coping with stress. This simple, potent exercise provides practical tools for focusing on what needs attention today. (20–30 min)
161 Affirmation Calendar	p. 71	Create a self-affirmation/esteem-building calendar and use it daily as an essential stress management tool. (25–30 min)
166 Five and Ten	p. 99	The simplicity of this quick assessment and planning process is what makes it so powerful. Use it with any group for a dynamite closing piece. (10–15 min)

ESPECIALLY FOR THE WORKPLACE

Most of the exercises in this volume are "generic" stress assessment or management processes that can be easily adapted to a variety of settings. Occasionally you may be asked to specifically address the issue of workplace stress. If so, the exercises outlined below will be particularly applicable.

©1995 Whole Person Press ₤10 W Michigan Duluth MN 55802   (800) 247-6789

WINNING COMBINATIONS

Coping with Stress: Managing Anger and Anxiety (1–2 hours)

For most people, anger and anxiety are typical stress responses—and frequent stress escalators. A skill-building workshop geared to help people manage these feelings would be appropriate for nearly any audience or setting.

Begin with a mood-setting warm-up, **One Minute Autobiographies** (Exercise 148, p. 10, 10–20 min). Direct folks to tell their life stories by focusing on episodes of anger or anxiety only.

Exercise 163, **Keep Your Cool** (p. 81, 60–90 min) vividly demonstrates how we can be directors rather than victims of our feelings. Although the exercise is geared toward managing anger, the process and content apply equally well to anxiety. You could choose a focus on one of these problems or combine both in a single session. Adapt the role play scenarios to generate the desired feeling(s). If time is limited, reduce the number of scenarios.

> Be sure to include **Remote Control** (Exercise 164, p. 91, 20–30 min). This vivid demonstration of people's power to regulate their moods and actions in unforgettable. If you have time, use the visualization in Exercise 179, **Trouble Bubbles** (p. 131, 5–10 min) as an additional demonstration of controlling anger or anxiety by relaxing and blowing away the negative feelings.

For an uplifting ending, try Exercise 167, **Go Fly a Kite** (p. 99, 10–20 min). Modify the questions to focus on the stress of anxiety or anger. Encourage everyone to create a plan for managing these feelings that is guaranteed to fly.

As a farewell ritual, create **Stress Squeezers** (Exercise 176, p. 124, 10–15 min) and encourage people to use these flexible toys as tools for releasing anxiety and anger by squeezing them whenever they start to feel stressed out.

Workshop on the Hardiness Factor (2–3 hours)

If you're tired of Selye's eustress/distress theory, Type A Behavior, and the stress of life change events, try a presentation or workshop that focuses on assessing and building stress resistance.

Start the workshop with a short group warm-up, using Exercise 147, **Nametag Questions** (p. 7, 15–20 min), tailoring the questions to hardiness issues. Modify the time as needed by varying the number of times people change partners.

The chalktalks and assessment in Exercise 151, **Hardiness Factor** (p. 17, 30–40 min) provide a broad introduction to Kobasa's research on stress resistance, and specific feedback to participants on their relative strength in the three hard-iness traits: challenge, commitment, and control.

©1995 Whole Person Press 210 W Michigan Duluth MN 55802   (800) 247-6789

◆ **Challenge**. Exercise 158, **Silver Linings** (p. 55, 20–30 min) is perfect for discovering opportunities (challenge) in stressful situations.

◆ **Commitment**. To expand on this topic use **Life and Death Questions** (*Wellness 2*, p. 85, 20–30 min with group sharing omitted) or **Expanding Your Circles** (*Wellness 4*, p. 71, 20–30 min).

◆ **Control**. Exercise 153, **Pick Your Battles** (p. 34, 30 min), or Exercise 160, **Yesterday, Today, Tomorrow** (p. 66, 20–30 min) address issues of control in stress management.

Exercise 180, **Try, Try Again** (p. 133, 5 min) or Exercise 174, **Hand Dancing** (p. 120, 10 min) provide playful energizers dealing with control and letting go.

◆ The concept of physical resilience can be introduced by Exercise 165, **Yoga**, (p. 94, 30–60 min), Exercise 173, **Cobra** (p. 118, 5 min), or Exercise 175, **Humming Breath** (p. 122, 3–5 min).

For planning and closure, Exercise 169, **Key Learning** (p. 108, 5–10 min) is well-suited. If you have other volumes of the **Structured Exercises** series, you can add more pizzazz to your workshop by substituting **Stress Buffer Shield** (**Stress 1**, p. 71, 20–30 min).

Superwoman Stress Workshop (2–4 hours)

Women comprise the largest segment of most audiences at stress management programs. If you'd like to address the special issues women face, build a workshop around Exercise 152, **Lifetrap 5: Superwoman Syndrome** (p. 22, 60–90 min).

Begin with Exercise 146, **Badge of My Profession** (p. 4, 15–20 min), adapting the worksheet questions to fit the role of Superwomen. Then proceed through the analysis of **Superwoman** stress (p. 23): myths, stress symptoms, guilt and expectations, entitlement, and strategies for change. Since low self-esteem is a chronic issue for so many women, incorporate Exercise 161, **Affirmation Calendar** (p. 71, 25–30 min) as a part of *Step 13*.

To expand the skill-building focus of your workshop, include Exercise 162, **Eating Under Stress** (p. 76, 40–45 min) or Exercise 165, **Yoga** (p. 94, 20–30 min), which are both superb skills for Superwomen.

Conclude with an affirming female systems process for gathering insights and resolutions: Exercise 168, **Hope Chest** (p. 105, 15–20 min).

Be sure to take frequent breaks—Superwomen tend to ignore their self-care needs.

◆ Exercise 177, **Superman** (p. 126, 5–10 min) is sure to get a laugh.

◆ Exercise 175, **Humming Breath** (p. 122, 3–5 min) and Exercise 172, **Breath Prayer** (p. 115, 5–15 min) are powerful energizers.

◆ If you have time, insert **Mealtime Meditation** (*Wellness 5*, p. 56, 10–15 min) before a lunch break.

ANNOTATED INDEXES

Index to CHALKTALKS

©1995 Whole Person Press 210 W Michigan Duluth MN 55802   (800) 247-6789

Index to DEMONSTRATIONS

Index to PHYSICAL ENERGIZERS

Index to MENTAL ENERGIZERS

Index to RELAXATION ROUTINES

©1995 Whole Person Press 210 W Michigan Duluth MN 55802   (800) 247-6789

CONTRIBUTORS

Martha Belknap, MA. 1170 Dixon Road, Gold Hill, Boulder CO 80302. 303/447-9642. Marti is an educational consultant with a specialty in creative relaxation and stress management skills. She has 30 years of teaching experience at all levels. Marti offers relaxation workshops and creativity courses through schools, universities, hospitals and businesses. She is the author of **Taming Your Dragons**, a book and cassette tape of creative relaxation activities for home and school.

Lyman Coleman, MDiv, PhD. Serendipity House, Box 1012, Littleton CO 80160. 303/798-1313. Founder and director of Serendipity Workshops, Lyman has spent the past 30 years training over 150,000 church leaders of all denominations in small group processes. Author of scores of books, including a small group discussion version of the Bible, Lyman's innovative approach combines Bible study, group building and values orientation with personal story telling.

David and Anne Frähm. Health*Quarters*, 6873 Prince Dr, Colorado Springs CO 80918. 719/593–8694. Dave and Anne are authors of **A Cancer Battle Plan** (1992), **Healthy Habits** (1993), and **Reclaim Your Health** (1994). Besides writing books about health issues, they are co-directors of Health*Quarters*, a non-profit health resource and information center and guest lodge.

Joel Goodman, EdD. Director, The HUMOR Project, 110 Spring Street, Saratoga Springs NY 12866. 518/587-8770. Joel is a popular speaker, consultant and seminar leader who has presented to over 600,000 corporate managers, health care leaders, educators, and other helping professionals throughout the U.S. and abroad. Author of eight books, including **Laffirmations: 1001 Ways to Add Humor to Your Life and Work**, Joel publishes **Laughing Matters** magazine and **HUMOResources** mail order bookstore catalog, and sponsors the annual international conference on "The Positive Power of Humor and Creativity."

Krysta Eryn Kavenaugh, MA, CSP. 955 Lake Drive, St. Paul MN 55120. 800/829-8437 (w) 612/725-6763 (h). Krysta is a speaker, trainer, and consultant. Her mission is to take people "into the heart of wisdom." She speaks with style, substance, and spirit. She is also the managing editor of **Marriage** magazine. Her favorite keynote topic is "Romancing Yourself: Taking Care of You is Taking Care of Business." She also speaks on proactive support teams, turning adversity to our advantage, ecology, and customized business topics.

Julie Lusk, MEd. Lewis-Gale Clinic, 1802 Braeburn Drive, Salem VA 24153. 703/772-3736. Julie is the editor of **30 Scripts for Relaxation, Imagery, and Inner Healing** (volumes 1 and 2). She works as the director of the Health Management Center at Lewis-Gale Clinic and is the founder of the Alive and Well Coalition in Roanoke VA. She leads workshops worldwide on a variety of topics and develops wellness programs for businesses, colleges, and communities. Julie is a licensed professional counselor and has taught Yoga since 1977.

Pat Miller, 1211 N Basswood Ave, Duluth MN 55811. 218/722-9361. Pat runs her own consulting and teaching business, Pat Miller Training and Development. She teaches workshops, conducts on-site team building sessions, facilitates retreats, and mediates conflict in the workplace. Her areas of expertise include communication skills, conflict resolution, team development, self-esteem, and stress management.

Price Pritchett, PhD. 13155 Noel Ct, Suite 1600, Dallas TX 75240. 214/789–7971. Price is the CEO of Pritchett & Associates Inc, a Dallas-based consulting firm specializing in organizational change. He has authored eleven books on individual and organizational effectiveness, including **You[2]: A High Velocity Formula for Multiplying Your Personal Effectiveness in Quantum Leaps, New Work Habits for a Radically Changing World**, and **The Employee's Survival Guide to the Stress of Organizational Change**.

Mary O'Brien Sippel, RN, MS. Licensed Psychologist, 22 East St. Andrews, Duluth MN 55803. 218/723-6130 (w) 218/724-5935 (h). Mary has spent over 25 years working the field of community health and education. Her experience in teaching stress management, burnout prevention, and wellness promotion across the country has enabled her to be her own best caretaker as career woman, wife, and mother of two teenagers. Mary is currently a personal counselor and adjunct faculty member at the College of St Scholastica, Duluth MN. She has ten publications to her credit, never tiring of sharing her enthusiasm for life both on paper and in front of her audiences.

David X Swenson, PhD. Assoc Professor of Management, College of St Scholastica, 1200 Kenwood Ave, Duluth MN 55811. 218/723-6476 (w) 218/525-3723 (h). A licensed consulting psychologist, Dave maintains a private practice in addition to his educational and therapeutic roles at the college. He provides consultation and training to human services, health and law enforcement agencies and is the author of **Stress Managment in the Criminal Justice System**. Dave also develops stress management software.

FUTURE CONTRIBUTORS

If you have developed an exciting, effective exercise you'd like to share with other trainers in the field of stress or wellness, please send it to us for consideration, using the following guidelines:

● Your entry should be written in a format similiar to those in this volume.

● Contributors must either guarantee that the materials they submit are not previously copyrighted or provide a copyright release for inclusion in the Whole Person **Structured Exercises** series.

● When you have adapted the work of others, please acknowledge the original source of ideas or activities.

EDITORS

All exercises in this volume not specifically attributed to other contributors are the creative efforts of the editors, who have been designing, collecting, and experimenting with structured processes in their teaching, training, and consultation work since the late 1960s.

Nancy Loving Tubesing, EdD, holds a masters degree in group counseling and a doctorate in counselor education. Faculty Associate and Product Development Director at Whole Person Associates, Nancy is co-author of two self-help books on whole person wellness, **The Caring Question** (Minneapolis: Augsburg, 1983) and **Seeking Your Healthy Balance** (Duluth: Whole Person Press, 1991) and a score of unusual relaxation audiotapes.

Nancy also collaborated with Don Tubesing in developing creative stress management programs and packages for client groups such as the national YMCA (8-session course, **The Y's Way to Stress Management**) and Aid Association for Lutherans (The Stress Kit multimedia resource for families).

Their most recent efforts have been directed toward combining the process-oriented approach of the **Structured Exercises** series with the power of video. The resulting three six-session interactive video courses, **WellAware**, **Manage It!**, and **Managing Job Stress**, include participant booklets with worksheets that stimulate personal reflection and application of principles to specific situations, as well as a step-by-step leader manual for guiding group interaction.

Sandy Stewart Christian, MSW, is a licensed independent clinical social worker and a licensed marriage and family therapist. Prior to joining the Product Development Team at Whole Person Associates in 1994, Sandy worked for nearly seventeen years as a therapist and clinical supervisor at a private counseling agency. She was on the behavioral science faculty at the Duluth Family Practice Center for over ten years and is an adjunct faculty member at the St. Mary's Hospital Chaplaincy program in Duluth, Minnesota. In her work as a therapist, teacher, trainer, and consultant, Sandy has maintained a lively whole person focus in health and stress management.

WORKSHOPS-IN-A-BOOK

The easy-to-understand, user-friendly format of Whole Person Workshops-in-a-Book are perfect for use as:
- a classroom text, discussion guide, or participant workbook;
- a professional resource for both novice and experienced trainers;
- a personal journey for individuals.

KICKING YOUR STRESS HABITS:
A Do-it-yourself Guide for Coping with Stress
Donald A. Tubesing, PhD

Over a quarter of a million people have found ways to deal with their everyday stress by using **Kicking Your Stress Habits**. This workshop-in-a-book actively involves the reader in assessing stressful patterns and developing more effective coping strategies with helpful "Stop and Reflect" sections in each chapter.

The 10-step planning process and 20 skills for managing stress make **Kicking Your Stress Habits** an ideal text for stress management classes in many different settings, from hospitals to universities.

Kicking Your Stress Habits / $14.95

SEEKING YOUR HEALTHY BALANCE:
A Do-it-yourself Guide to Whole Person Well-Being
Donald A. Tubesing, PhD and Nancy Loving Tubesing, EdD

Where can people find the time and energy to "do it all" without sacrificing health and well-being? **Seeking Your Healthy Balance** helps readers discover how to develop a more balanced lifestyle by learning effective ways to juggle work, self, and others; by clarifying self-care options; and by discovering and setting personal priorities.

Seeking Your Healthy Balance asks the questions that help readers find their own answers as they pursue the path to wellness.

Seeking Your Healthy Balance / $14.95

To order, call toll free   (800) 247-6789

©1995 Whole Person Press 210 W Michigan Duluth MN 55802   (800) 247-6789

STRUCTURED EXERCISES
IN STRESS MANAGEMENT—VOLUMES 1–5

Nancy Loving Tubesing, EdD, Donald A. Tubesing, PhD,
and Sandy Stewart Christian, MSW, Editors

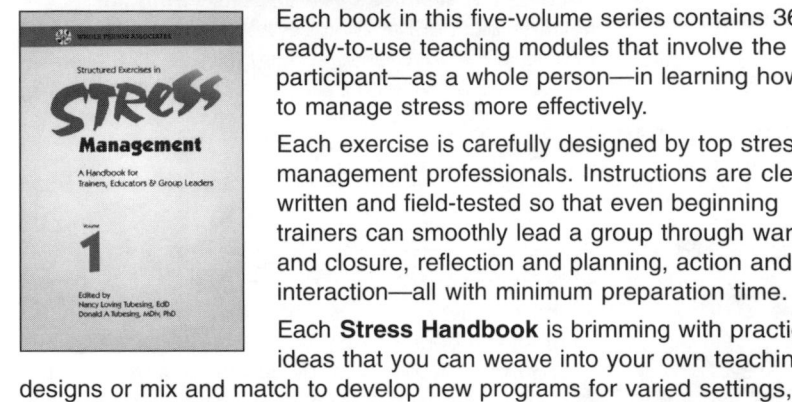

Each book in this five-volume series contains 36 ready-to-use teaching modules that involve the participant—as a whole person—in learning how to manage stress more effectively.

Each exercise is carefully designed by top stress-management professionals. Instructions are clearly written and field-tested so that even beginning trainers can smoothly lead a group through warm-up and closure, reflection and planning, action and interaction—all with minimum preparation time.

Each **Stress Handbook** is brimming with practical ideas that you can weave into your own teaching designs or mix and match to develop new programs for varied settings, audiences, and time frames. In each volume you'll find **Icebreakers, Stress Assessments, Management Strategies, Skill Builders, Action Planners, Closing Processes,** and **Group Energizers**—all with a special focus on stress management.

> **Stress 8 1/2" x 11" Loose-Leaf Edition—Volumes 1–5 / $54.95 per volume**
> Includes Worksheet Masters (see below).
> **Stress 6" x 9" Softcover Edition—Volumes 1–5 / $29.95 per volume**

STRUCTURED EXERCISES WORKSHEET MASTERS

The Worksheet Masters for the stress and wellness **Structured Exercises** series offer full-size (8 1/2" x 11") photocopy masters. All of the worksheets and handouts for each volume are reproduced in easy-to-read print with professional graphics. All you need to do to complete your workshop preparation is run them through a copier.

Worksheet Masters are automatically included with the Loose-Leaf Editions.

> **Structured Exercises in Stress Management Volumes 1–5**
> **Worksheet Masters / $9.95 per volume**
>
> **Structured Exercises in Wellness Promotion Volumes 1–5**
> **Worksheet Masters / $9.95 per volume**

To order, call toll free   (800) 247-6789

©1995 Whole Person Press 210 W Michigan Duluth MN 55802   (800) 247-6789

STRUCTURED EXERCISES
IN WELLNESS PROMOTION—VOLUMES 1–5

Nancy LovingTubesing, EdD, Donald A.Tubesing, PhD,
and Sandy Stewart Christian, MSW, Editors

Discover the **Wellness Handbooks**—from the wellness pioneers at Whole Person Associates. Each volume in this innovative series includes 36 experiential learning activities that focus on whole person health—body, mind, spirit, emotions, relationships, and lifestyle.

The exercises, developed by an interdisciplinary pool of leaders in the wellness movement nationwide, actively encourage people to adopt wellness-oriented attitudes and to develop more responsible self-care patterns.

All process designs in the Wellness Handbooks are clearly explained and have been thoroughly field-tested with diverse audiences so that trainers can use them with confidence. **Icebreakers, Wellness Explorations, Self-Care Strategies, Action Planners, Closings,** and **Group Energizers** are all ready-to-go—including reproducible worksheets, scripts, and chalktalk outlines—for the busy professional who wants to develop unique wellness programs without spending hours in preparation.

> **Wellness 8 1/2" x 11" Loose-Leaf Edition—Volumes 1–5 / $54.95 per volume**
> Includes Worksheet Masters (see p. 154)
> **Wellness 6" x 9" Softcover Edition—Volumes 1–5 / $29.95 per volume**

STRESS AND WELLNESS REFERENCE GUIDE
A Comprehensive Index to the Chalktalks, Processes, and Activites in the Whole Person Structured Exercises Series
Nancy LovingTubesing, EdD

This handy index is your key to over 360 teaching designs of the ten volumes of the **Stress and Wellness Handbook** series—organized by theme, time frame, level of self-disclosure, trainer experience level, and goals. The book includes the *Tips for Trainers* sections for all ten books, with workshop outlines and suggested processes especially for the workplace—as well as annotated listings of all chalktalks, demonstrations, physical and mental energizers, relaxation techniques, and the editors' choice of favorite exercises.

The **Index** makes it easy to plan a workshop by mixing and matching exercises suitable to your audience. You'll find easy-to-read charts with a quick view of goals, times, group processes and activities—so you can find your favorites to use with any group.

> **Stress and Wellness Reference Guide / $29.95**

©1995 Whole Person Press 210 W Michigan Duluth MN 55802   (800) 247 6790

ADDITIONAL GROUP PROCESS RESOURCES

Our group process exercises are designed to address the whole person—physical, emotional, mental, spiritual, and social. Developed for trainers by trainers, all of these topical group process resources are ready-to-use. Novice trainers will find everything they need to get started, and the expert trainer will discover new ideas and concepts to add to existing programs.

All of the exercises encourage interaction between the leader and the participants, as well as among the participants. Each exercise includes everything you need to present a meaningful program: goals, optimal group size, time frame, materials list, and complete process instructions.

PLAYFUL ACTIVITIES FOR
POWERFUL PRESENTATIONS
Bruce Williamson

This book contains 40 fun exercises designed to fit any group or topic. These exercises will help you:

• build teamwork
• encourage laughter and playfulness
• relieve stress and tension
• free up the imagination of participants

Playful Activities for Powerful Presentations $19.95

WORKING WITH GROUPS FROM
DYSFUNCTIONAL FAMILIES
Cheryl Hetherington

This collection of 29 proven group activities is designed to heal the pain that results from living in a dysfunctional family. With these exercises you can:

• promote healing • build self-esteem
• encourage sharing
• help participants acknowledge their feelings.

**Working with Groups from
Dysfunctional Families / $24.95**

WORKSHEET MASTERS
A complete package of (8 1/2" x 11") photocopy masters is available for **Working with Groups from Dysfunctional Families**. Use the masters to conveniently duplicate handouts for each participant.

**Working with Groups from Dysfunctional Families
Worksheet Masters / $9.95**

©1995 Whole Person Press 210 W Michigan Duluth MN 55802   (800) 247-6789

WORKING WITH WOMEN'S GROUPS VOLUMES 1 & 2
Louise Yolton Eberhardt

The two volumes of **Working with Women's Groups** have been completely revised and updated. These exercises will help women explore issues that are of perennial concern as well as today's hot topics.

* consciousness-raising (volume 1)
* self-discovery (volume 1)
* assertiveness training (volume 1)
* sexuality issues (volume 2)
* women of color (volume 2)
* leadership skills training (volume 2)
    Working with Women's Groups Volume 1 / $24.95
    Working with Women's Groups Volume 2 / $24.95

WORKING WITH MEN'S GROUPS
Roger Karsk and Bill Thomas

Also revised and updated, this volume is a valuable resource for anyone working with men's groups. The exercises cover a variety of topics, including:

* self discovery • parenting • conflict • intimacy
    Working with Men's Groups / $24.95

WELLNESS ACTIVITIES FOR YOUTH VOLUMES 1 & 2
Sandy Queen

Each volume of **Wellness Activities for Youth** help leaders touch children and teenagers about wellness with an emphasis on FUN. The concepts include:

* values • stress and coping • self-esteem
* personal well-being
    Wellness Activities for Youth Volume 1 / $24.95
    Wellness Activities for Youth Volume 2 / $24.95

WORKSHEET MASTERS
Complete packages of full-size (8 1/2" x 11") photocopy masters that include all worksheets and handouts are available to you. Use the masters for easy duplication of the handouts for each participant.

    Working with Women's Groups V. 1 & 2 Worksheet Masters / $9.95 each volume
    Working with Men's Groups Worksheet Masters / $9.95
    Wellness Activities for Youth V. 1 & 2 Worksheet Masters / $9.95 each volume

©1995 Whole Person Press 210 W Michigan Duluth MN 55802   (800) 247-6789

WORKING WITH GROUPS IN THE WORKPLACE

CONFRONTING SEXUAL HARASSMENT
Louise Yolten Eberhardt

Preventing sexual harassment requires more than just enforcing the laws—changing attitudes is just as crucial. **Confronting Sexual Harassment** contains a wealth of exercises that trainers can safely use with groups to constructively explore the issue, look at the underlying causes, understand the law, motivate men to become allies, and empower women to speak up. It's a valuable tool for private employers, government agencies, schools, religious institutions, and nonprofit organizations.

> **Confronting Sexual Harassment / $24.95**

BRIDGING THE GENDER GAP
Louise Yolten Eberhardt

Bridging the Gender Gap contains 37 exercises for the trainer to use in team building, gender role awareness groups, diversity training, couples workshops, college classes, or youth seminars. The exercises encourage participants to examine gender stereotypes and attitudes, discover the effects of these attitudes, and form a shared consciousness for both genders so they can humanize their roles, relationships, and personal lives.

> **Bridging the Gender Gap / $24.95**

To order, call toll free   (800) 247-6789

©1995 Whole Person Press 210 W Michigan Duluth MN 55802   (800) 247-6789

CELEBRATING DIVERSITY
Cheryl Hetherington

Celebrating Diversity helps people confront and question the beliefs, prejudices, and fears that can separate them from others. The 28 exercises provide valuable assistance to trainers leading groups in evaluating past experiences, exploring negative feelings, and beginning a journey toward truly celebrating the differences that unite us.

Celebrating Diversity / $24.95

WORKING WITH GROUPS ON SPIRITUAL THEMES
Structured Exercises in Healing
Elaine Hopkins, Zo Woods, Russell Kelly,
Katrina Bentley, James Murphy

Whether spirituality is the focus of your group or is one of many issues being explored, you will find creative ideas in **Working with Groups on Spiritual Themes** that will help you initiate discussion and promote healing and personal growth. The 39 exercise are particularly effective with groups who want to explore the meaning and purpose of life. Use this book for:

• personal growth groups • hospitals
• retreat centers • mental health facilities
• church groups • nursing homes

Spiritual Themes / $24.95

WORKSHEET MASTERS
A complete package of full-size (8 1/2" x 11") photocopy masters that includes all the worksheets and the key handouts from **Working with Groups** is available to you. Use the masters for easy duplication of the worksheets for each participant.

Confronting Sexual Harassment Worksheets / $9.95
Bridging the Gender Gap Worksheets / $9.95
Celebrating Diversity Worksheets / $9.95
Spiritual Themes Worksheets / $9.95

©1995 Whole Person Press 210 W Michigan Duluth MN 55802   (800) 247-6789

RELAXATION AUDIOTAPES

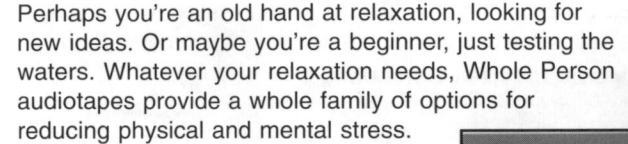

Perhaps you're an old hand at relaxation, looking for new ideas. Or maybe you're a beginner, just testing the waters. Whatever your relaxation needs, Whole Person audiotapes provide a whole family of options for reducing physical and mental stress.

Techniques range from simple breathing and stretching exercises to classic autogenic and progressive relaxation sequences, guided meditations, and whimsical daydreams. All are carefully crafted to promote whole person relaxation—body, mind, and spirit.

If you're looking for an extended relaxation experience (20 minutes or more), try a tape from the *Sensational Relaxation, Guided Imagery,* or *Wilderness Daydreams* groups. For quick R&R breaks (5–10 minutes), try a *Stress Breaks, Daydreams,* or *Mini-Meditations* collections. All of our tapes feature male and female narrators.

Audiotapes are available for $11.95 each.
Call for generous quantity discounts.

SENSATIONAL RELAXATION—$11.95 each
When stress piles up, it becomes a heavy load both physically and emotionally. These full-length relaxation experiences will teach you techniques that can be used whenever you feel that stress is getting out of control. Choose one you like and repeat it daily until it becomes second nature, then recall that technique whenever you need it—or try a new one every day.

> **Countdown to Relaxation /** Countdown 19:00, Staircase 19:00
> **Daybreak / Sundown /** Daybreak 22:00, Sundown 22:00
> **Take a Deep Breath /** Breathing for Relaxation 17:00, Magic Ball 17:00
> **Relax . . . Let Go . . . Relax /** Revitalization 27:00, Relaxation 28:00
> **StressRelease /** Quick Tension Relievers 22:00,Progressive Relaxation 20:00
> **Warm and Heavy /** Warm 24:00, Heavy 23:00

STRESS BREAKS—$11.95 each
Do you need a short energy booster or a quick stress reliever? If you don't know what type of relaxation you like, or if you are new to guided relaxation techniques, try one of our *Stress Breaks* for a quick refocusing or change of pace any time of the day.

> **BreakTime /** Solar Power 8:00, Belly Breathing 9:00, Fortune Cookie 9:00,
>   Mother Earth 11:00, Big Yawn 5:00,Affirmation 11:00
> **Natural Tranquilizers /** Clear the Deck 10:00, Body Scan 10:00,
>   99 Countdown 10:00, Calm Down 9:00, Soothing Colors 11:00,
>   Breathe Ten 9:00
> **Effortless Relaxation /** Sensory Relaxation 16:00, Breathe Away Tension 8:00,
>   Anchoring 8:00, Breathing Meditation 7:00, Pulling Strings 4:00,
>   Groans and Moans 5:00

©1995 Whole Person Press 210 W Michigan Duluth MN 55802   (800) 247-6789

DAYDREAMS—$11.95 each
Escape from the stress around you with guided tours to beautiful places. The quick escapes in our *Daydreams* tapes will lead your imagination away from your everyday cares so you can resume your tasks relaxed and comforted.

Daydreams 1: Getaways / Cabin Retreat 11:00, Night Sky 10:00, Hot Spring 7:00, Mountain View 8:00, Superior Sail 8:00

Daydreams 2: Peaceful Places / Ocean Tides 11:00, City Park 10:00, Hammock 8:00, Meadow 11:00

Daydreams 3: Relaxing Retreats / Melting Candle 5:00, Tropical Paradise 10:00, Sanctuary 7:00, Floating Clouds 5:00, Seasons 9:00, Beach Tides 9:00

GUIDED MEDITATION—$11.95 each
Take a step beyond relaxation. The imagery in our full-length meditations will help you discover your strengths, find healing, make positive life changes, and recognize your inner wisdom.

Inner Healing / Inner Healing 20:00, Peace with Pain 20:00

Personal Empowering / My Gifts 22:00, Hidden Strengths 21:00

Healthy Balancing / Inner Harmony 20:00, Regaining Equilibrium 20:00

Spiritual Centering / Spiritual Centering 20:00 (male and female narration)

WILDERNESS DAYDREAMS—$11.95 each
Discover the healing power of nature with the four tapes in our *Wilderness Daydreams* series. These eight special journeys will transport you from your harried, stressful surroundings to the peaceful serenity of words and water.

Canoe / Rain / Canoe 19:00, Rain 22:00

Island / Spring / Island 19:00, Spring 19:00

Campfire / Stream / Campfire 17:00, Stream 19:00

Sailboat / Pond / Sailboat 25:00, Pond 25:00

MINI-MEDITATIONS—$11.95 each
These brief guided visualizations begin by focusing your breathing and uncluttering your mind, so that you can concentrate on a sequence of sensory images that promote relaxation, centering, healing, growth, and spiritual awareness.

Healing Visions / Rocking Chair 5:00, Pine Forest 8:00, Long Lost Confidant 10:00, Caterpillar to Butterfly 7:00, Superpowers 9:00, Tornado 8:00

Refreshing Journeys / 1 to 10 10:00, Thoughts Library 11:00, Visualizing Change 6:00, Magic Carpet 9:00, Pond of Love 9:00, Cruise 9:00

Healthy Choices / Lifestyle 6:00, Eating 5:00, Exercise 3:00, Stress 5:00, Relationships 6:00, Change 7:00

MUSIC ONLY—$11.95 each
No relaxation program would be complete without relaxing melodies that can be played as background to a prepared script or that can be enjoyed as you practice a technique you have already learned. Steven Eckels composed his melodies specifically for relaxation. These "musical prayers for healing" will calm your body, mind, and spirit.

Tranquility / Awakening 20:00, Repose 20:00

Harmony / Waves of Light 30:00, Rising Mist 10:00, Frankincense 10:00, Angelica 10:00

Serenity / Radiance 20:00, Quiessence 10:00, Evanesence 10:00

©1995 Whole Person Press 210 W Michigan Duluth MN 55802   (800) 247 0700

RELAXATION RESOURCES

Many trainers and workshop leaders have discovered the benefits of relaxation and visualization in healing the body, mind, and spirit.

30 SCRIPTS FOR RELAXATION, IMAGERY, AND INNER HEALING
Julie Lusk

The relaxation scripts, creative visualizations, and guided meditations in these volumes were created by experts in the field of guided imagery. Julie Lusk collected their best and most effective scripts to help novices get started and experienced leaders expand their repertoire. Both volumes include information on how to use the scripts, suggestions for tailoring them to specific needs and audiences, and information on how to successfully incorporate guided imagery into existing programs.

30 Scripts / Volume 1 & 2 / $19.95 each

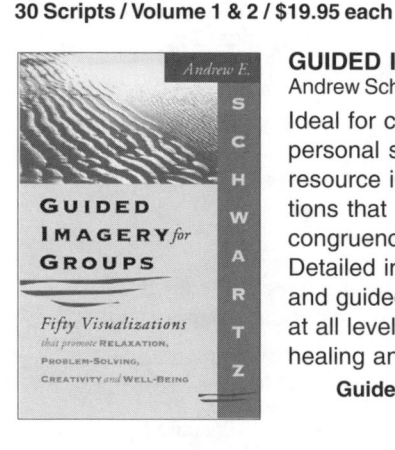

GUIDED IMAGERY FOR GROUPS
Andrew Schwartz

Ideal for courses, workshops, team building, and personal stress management, this comprehensive resource includes scripts for 50 thematic visualizations that promote calming, centering, creativity, congruence, clarity, coping, and connectedness. Detailed instructions for using relaxation techniques and guided images in group settings allow educators at all levels, in any setting, to help people tap into the healing and creative powers of imagery.

Guided Imagery for Groups / $24.95

INQUIRE WITHIN
Andrew Schwartz

Use visualization to help people make positive changes in their life. The 24 visualization experiences in **Inquire Within** will help participants enhance their creativity, heal inner pain, learn to relax, and deal with conflict. Each visualization includes questions at the end of the process that encourage deeper reflection and a better understanding of the exercise and the response it evokes.

Inquire Within / $19.95

©1995 Whole Person Press 210 W Michigan Duluth MN 55802   (800) 247-6789

ABOUT WHOLE PERSON ASSOCIATES

At Whole Person Associates, we're 100% committed
to providing stress and wellness materials that involve
participants and provide a "whole person" focus—
body, mind, spirit, and relationships.

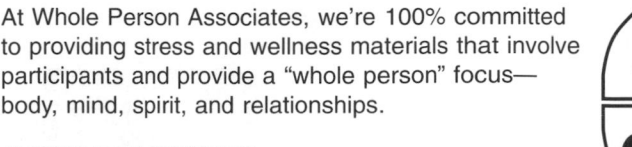

ABOUT THE OWNERS
Whole Person Associates was created by the vision of
two people: Donald A. Tubesing, PhD, and Nancy Loving
Tubesing, EdD. Don and Nancy have been active in the stress
management/wellness promotion movement for over twenty years—
consulting, leading seminars, writing, and publishing. Most of our early
products were the result of their creativity and expertise. Living proof that
you can "stay evergreen," Don and Nancy remain the driving force behind
the company and are still active in developing new products that touch
people's lives.

ABOUT THE COMPANY
Whole Person Associates was "born" in Duluth, Minnesota, and we remain
committed to our lovely city on the shore of Lake Superior. We put the same
high quality into every product we offer, translating the best of current
research into practical, accessible, easy-to-use materials. We create the
best possible resources to help our customers teach about stress management and wellness promotion. And our friendly and resourceful employees
are committed to helping you find the products that fit your needs.

ABOUT OUR ASSOCIATES
Who are the "associates" in Whole Person Associates? They're the trainers,
authors, musicians, and others who have developed much of the material
you see on these pages. We're always on the lookout for high-quality
products that reflect our "whole person" philosophy and fill a need for our
customers. Our products were developed by experts who are at the top of
their fields, and we're very proud to be associated with them.

ABOUT OUR RELATIONSHIP TO YOU
We'd love to hear from you! Let us know what you think of our
products—how you use them in your work, what additional products you'd
like to see, and what shortcomings you've noted. Write us or call on our toll-
free line. We look forward to hearing from you!

To order, call toll free   (800) 247-6789

©1995 Whole Person Press 210 W Michigan Duluth MN 55802   (800) 247-6789